Ru
for Pharmaceutic
Distributors 2015

Rules and Guidance for Pharmaceutical Distributors 2015

Compiled by the Inspection, Enforcement and Standards Division of MHRA

Published by Pharmaceutical Press

1 Lambeth High Street, London SE1 7JN, UK

© Crown Copyright 2015

Medicines and Healthcare
Products Regulatory Agency

MHRA, a center of the Medicines and Healthcare Products Regulatory Agency
151 Buckingham Palace Road
Victoria
London SW1W 9SZ
Information on re-use of crown copyright information can be found on MHRA
website: www.mhra.gov.uk

Designed and published by Pharmaceutical Press 2015

(**PP**) is a trade mark of Pharmaceutical Press

Pharmaceutical Press is the publishing division of the Royal Pharmaceutical Society

First edition published in 2007, second edition 2014, third edition 2015
Reprinted 2015

Typeset by OKS Group, Chennai, India
Printed in Great Britain by Berforts Infomation Press Ltd, Oxford, UK
Index Provided by Indexing Specialists, Hove, UK.

ISBN 978 0 85711 172 2 (print)
ISBN 978 0 85711 206 4 (ePDF)
ISBN 978 0 85711 207 1 (mobi)
ISBN 978 0 85711 208 8 (ePub)

Contents

MHRA   1

Legislation on Manufacture and Importation   37

3   EU Legislation on Manufacture and Importation   39

4   UK Legislation on the Manufacture, Importation and Distribution of Active Substances   44

Guidance on Wholesale Distribution Practice and Brokering Medicines   53

5   Guidelines on Good Distribution Practice of Medicinal Products for Human Use (2013/C 343/01)   55

Preface to the 2015 edition

This 2015 edition of Rules and Guidance for Pharmaceutical Distributors (the "Green Guide") has been updated to incorporate the revised EU Guidelines on Good Distribution Practice and an updated section on product recall/withdrawal. In addition to these updates there are also new sections on:

- the Gold Standard for Responsible Persons
- MHRA Innovation Office
- the application and inspection process for new licences "what to expect"
- MHRA Compliance Management and Inspection Action Group
- MHRA risk-based inspection programme
- GDP quality systems
- sales representative samples
- handling returns of non-defective medicinal products
- short term storage of ambient and refrigerated medicinal products – requirements for a wholesale dealer's licence and
- controls on certain medicinal products.

There are also two added appendices on:

- the European Commission Q&A on GDP guidelines and
- a list of persons who can be supplied with medicines by way of wholesale dealing.

There is also a new flow chart on registration requirements for UK companies involved in the sourcing and supply of active substances (ASs) to be used in the manufacture of licensed human medicines.

Changes to the Community Code

The Falsified Medicines Directive 2011/62/EU amends Directive 2001/83/EC in a number of places. The first tranche of these changes in relation to manufacturing, wholesale dealing, supervision and sanctions came into force from 2 January 2013 with others relating to the importation of active substances from countries outside of the EEA taking effect from the 2 July

2013. These provisions are implemented in the United Kingdom by Regulations amending the Human Medicines Regulations 2012. Several other requirements, such as the matters relating to safety features, are still to transpose as they rely on additional regulations and guidance from the European Commission which are being developed.

The headline changes are as follows:

- The current regulatory expectation for the manufacturer of the medicinal product to have audited their suppliers of active substances for compliance with the relevant GMP has been formalised, as is the requirement for the written confirmation of audit (the "QP Declaration", currently required as part of the marketing authorisation application). This audit may be undertaken by the manufacturer of the medicinal product, or by a suitable and appropriately experienced third party under contract to the manufacturer of the medicinal product.
- In addition a formal requirement for manufacturers of medicinal products (or a third party acting under contract) to audit their suppliers of active substances for compliance with the requirements of Good Distribution Practice (GDP) particular to active substances has also been introduced.
- A new requirement for manufacturers, importers and distributors of active substances to be registered with the competent authority of the Member State in which they are established (in the UK this is MHRA). Registrations will be entered onto a database operated by the European Medicines Agency, in a similar manner to the EudraGMDP database. The manufacturer of the medicinal product must verify that their suppliers of active substances are registered.
- The regulatory expectation that manufacturers of the medicinal product will verify the authenticity and quality of the active substances and excipients they use has been formalised.
- The manufacture of active substances for use in a licensed medicinal product must be in compliance with the relevant GMP. These standards are currently described in Part II of the EU Guidelines on GMP.
- Active substances imported from outside of the EEA must have been manufactured in accordance with standards of GMP, at least equivalent to those in the EU and from the 2 July 2013 must be accompanied by a written confirmation that equivalent GMP standards and supervision apply in the exporting country, unless the active substance is sourced from a country, listed by the European Commission or exceptionally and where necessary, to ensure availability of medicinal products an EU GMP certificate for the site of manufacture is available.

- Manufacturers of medicinal products are required to assess the risk to product quality presented by any excipients they use, by way of a formalised documented risk assessment, and ascertain the appropriate good manufacturing practices necessary to assure their safety and quality. There is no explicit obligation for the medicinal product manufacturer to audit their suppliers of excipients, but it does require the manufacturer to assure themselves that the appropriate good manufacturing practices are being applied.
- In support of the above changes the European Commission is to adopt the following by means of delegated acts and guidelines:
  - principles and guidelines for GMP for active substances;
  - GDP guidelines for active substances; and
  - guidelines for the formal risk assessment process for excipients.
- New obligations on medicinal product manufacturers, wholesale distributors and brokers to inform the competent authority and the marketing authorisation holder (MAH) should information be obtained that products either manufactured under the scope of the manufacturing authorisation or received or offered may be falsified, whether those products are being distributed through the legitimate supply chain, or by illegal means.
- The introduction of the concept of brokering for finished medicinal products and associated obligations to comply with the applicable aspects of GDP.
- A new requirement for persons undertaking the wholesale distribution of medicinal products to third countries to hold an authorisation and to check that their customers are authorised to receive medicines. Where the medicinal products for export have been imported from a third country checks must also be made to ensure the supplier is authorised to supply medicines.
- An extension of the requirement to notify MHRA and the MAH where a wholesale dealer imports from another EEA Member State into the UK a medicinal product which is the subject of a marketing authorisation, and the importer is not the MAH or acting on the MAH's behalf, to centrally authorised products (those holding a marketing authorisation granted by the European Medicines Agency), and the introduction of the option for the competent authority to charge a fee for processing the notification. For products imported into the UK the competent authority would be either the European Medicines Agency or MHRA, depending on whether the product is centrally-authorised or not.

UK legislation

The Human Medicines Regulations 2012 [SI 2012/1916] which came into force on 14 August 2012 modernises the UK's medicines legislation. It replaces most of the 1968 Medicines Act and over 200 statutory instruments, which had been cluttering up the statute book and complicating the law. This consolidated medicines legislation conjoins the statutory provisions for all licences, authorisations and registrations for human medicines.

Changes on the horizon

- The new requirements introduced by the Falsified Medicines Directive for medicinal products to bear safety features (set out below) are to be the subject of a separate delegated act from the European Commission, and any standards for the use of them are still to be defined.
  - the Qualified Person to ensure that they have been affixed.
  - safety features not to be removed or covered unless the manufacturing authorisation holder verifies that the medicinal product is authentic and has not been tampered with and that replacement safety features are equivalent and are applied in accordance with GMP.
  - wholesale dealers to verify that any medicinal products they receive are not falsified, by checking that any "safety features" used on the outer packaging of a product are intact.
  - brokers and wholesale dealers to record the batch numbers of, as a minimum, those products with safety features attached and for wholesale dealers to provide a record of batch numbers when supplying those products to their customers.
- New guidelines, based on requirements in 2011/62/EU, on the principles of GDP for active substances for medicinal products for human use.

The Green Guide 2015

In the 2014 edition I reported that going forward, to keep up with changes to EU text and national provisions the print version of the *Rules & Guidance for Pharmaceutical Distributors* known as the Green Guide will be revised and published annually.

I am pleased to report that this is the first annual update of the Green Guide and is the third edition of the "Rules & Guidance for Pharmaceutical Distributors" issued by MHRA. This revised edition continues to bring together existing and revised Commission written material concerning the distribution and brokering of human medicines and matters relating to the manufacture, importation and distribution of active substances.

Although it is UK legislation, implementing the Directives, that bears directly on activities in the UK, it is often helpful for wholesalers to be aware of the original EU obligations. This is particularly so when trading across boundaries of Member States. Therefore, the "Titles" or sections of Directive 2001/83/EC, as amended, dealing with wholesale distribution of products for human use, brokering finished medicinal products and provisions relating to the manufacture, importation and distribution of active substances remain in this edition.

In this edition the revised EU Guidelines on Good Distribution Practice are included as well as an updated section on product recall/withdrawal. There are new sections covering MHRA's Innovation Office, Compliance Management and Inspection Action Group, and risk-based inspection programme.There are also additional sections on "what to expect" from the application and inspection process for new licences and updated UK guidance for wholesale dealers with new sections on GDP quality systems, sales representative samples, handling returns of non-defective medicinal products, short term storage of ambient and refrigerated medicinal products and controls on certain medicinal products.

Following extensive discussion with pharmaceutical companies and MHRA, Cogent (the national skills body for the science industries) has published a new Gold Standard role profile for the Responsible Person. This is included in this edition.

UK guidance and legislation for the brokering of finished medicinal products and the manufacture, importation and distribution of active substances remain and a new flow chart has been included for registration to manufacture, import and distribute active substances.

There are also two added appendices: the European Commission Q&A on GDP guidelines, and a list of persons who can be supplied with medicines by way of wholesale dealing.

Although much of the text in this book is available in its original form in other places, including various websites, I am pleased that the Green Guide continues to satisfy a demand for information in one authoritative and convenient place. The 2015 version will be available online, as part of "Medicines Complete" – a subscription-based database of leading medicines and healthcare references and in other electronic formats including other E-reader formats. I hope that this revised edition in its existing formats will continue to be useful.

Gerald Heddell
Director, Inspection, Enforcement and Standards Division
September 2014

Acknowledgements

To the European Commission for permission to reproduce the 1995–2014 text of the Directives, (Only European Union legislation printed in the paper edition of the Official Journal of the European Union is deemed authentic) and the guidelines on Good Distribution Practice and associated Q&A.

To the Heads of Medicines Agencies for permission to reproduce the names and addresses of other human and veterinary medicines authorities in Europe.

To Cogent for permission to reproduce the new Gold Standard role profile for the Responsible Person.

Feedback

Comments on the content or presentation of the Green Guide are encouraged and will be used to develop further editions. Your views are valued and both MHRA and Pharmaceutical Press would appreciate you taking the time to contact us. Please visit the feedback page at http://www.pharmpress.com/orangeguide-feedback or send your feedback to the address below:

"The Rules and Guidance for Pharmaceutical Distributors 2015"
Customer Services
MHRA
151 Buckingham Palace Road
Victoria
London SW1W 9SZ
UK
Tel.: +44 (0)20 3080 6000
Fax: +44 (0)20 3118 9803
E-mail: orange.guide@mhra.gsi.gov.uk

Introduction

The distribution network for medicinal products has become increasingly complex and now involves many different players.

The obligation on governments of all Member States of the European Union and European Economic Area (EEA)[1] to ensure that pharmaceutical wholesale distributors are authorised is stated in Title VII of the Directive 2001/83/EC. This Title requires all authorised wholesale distributors to have available a Responsible Person (RP) and to comply with the Commission guidelines on Good Distribution Practice (GDP).

Title VII Directive 2001/83/EC has been amended as a result of the Falsified Medicines Directive 2011/62/EU and now requires brokers of medicines within the Community to be registered with their competent authority and to comply with appropriate GDP requirements. Amended Title IV of the Directive 2001/83/EC also requires importers, manufacturers and distributors of active substances who are established in the Union to register their activity with the competent authority of the Member State in which they are established.

The Commission guidelines for GDP first issued in 1993 has been revised as a consequence of the Falsified Medicines Directive to assist wholesale distributors in conducting their activities and to prevent falsified medicines from entering the legal supply chain. The revised guidelines also provides specific rules for persons involved in activities in relation to the sale or purchase of medicinal products whilst not conducting a wholesale activity i.e. brokers of medicines.

In the United Kingdom, the provisions for wholesale distributors, brokers of medicines and manufacturers, importers and distributors of active substances have been implemented by requirements and undertakings incorporated in the Human Medicines Regulations 2012 [SI 2012/1916]. Through these regulations compliance by wholesale distributors and brokers of medicines with the Commission guidelines of GDP is a statutory requirement.

---

[1] The member states of the European Community plus Iceland, Liechtenstein and Norway.

This publication brings together the new Commission guidelines on GDP, UK guidance on wholesale distribution practice and EU and UK legislation on wholesale distribution, which wholesale distributors are expected to follow when distributing medicinal products for human use. It is of particular relevance to authorised wholesale distributors and to their RPs, who have a responsibility for ensuring compliance with many of these regulatory requirements. Wholesale distributors are required to appoint an RP who has the knowledge and responsibility to ensure that correct procedures are followed during distribution. Updated notes on the qualifications and duties of RPs are included in this publication to assist this.

This publication is also of particular relevance to all brokers of medicines because it brings together UK guidance on brokering medicines and EU and UK legislation on brokering, which brokers are expected to follow when brokering medicinal products for human use.

It is also of relevance to importers and distributors of active substances. The manufacture of active substances for use in a licensed medicinal product must be in compliance with the relevant good manufacturing practice. These standards are currently described in Part II of the EU Commission Guidelines on Good Manufacturing Practice (GMP). Active substances imported from outside of the EEA must have been manufactured in accordance with standards of GMP at least equivalent to those in the EU. From the 2 July 2013 they must be accompanied by a written confirmation that equivalent GMP standards and supervision apply in the exporting country, unless the active substance is sourced from a country listed by the European Commission or exceptionally and where necessary to ensure availability of medicinal products an EU GMP certificate for the site of manufacture is available.

The European Commission will be adopting principles and guidelines for GMP for active substances, GDP guidelines for active substances and guidelines for the formal risk assessment process for excipients by means of delegated acts and guidelines.

This guide brings together UK guidance and EU and UK legislation on the importation and distribution of active substances, which importers and distributors of active substances are expected to follow when supplying active substances for use in licensed medicinal products for human use. For completeness this guide also includes matters on what manufacturers of active substances have to comply with in order to provide further background information for importers and distributors of active substances.

The aim of GMP and GDP is to assure the quality of the medicinal product for the safety, well-being and protection of the patient. In achieving this aim it is impossible to over-emphasise the importance of individuals, at all levels, in the assurance of the quality of medicinal products. This is emphasised in the first principle in the EC Guide to GMP. The great majority of reported defective medicinal products has resulted from human error or carelessness, not from failures in technology. All individuals involved with the distribution of medicinal products should bear this constantly in mind when performing their duties.

Glossary of Legislation

European Legislation

Council Directive 2001/83/EC on the Community code relating to medicinal products for human use

This legislation regulates the licensing, manufacture of and wholesale dealing in medicinal products and registration, brokering of medicinal products and manufacture, importation and distribution of active substances within the European Community.

Council Directive 2003/94/EC laying down the principles and guidelines of good manufacturing practice in respect of medicinal products for human use and investigational medicinal products

This Directive lays down the principles and guidelines of good manufacturing practice in respect of medicinal products for human use whose manufacture requires an authorisation.

UK Legislation

The Human Medicines Regulations 2012 (SI 2012/1916)

The Regulations set out a comprehensive regime for the authorisation of medicinal products for human use; for the manufacture, import, distribution, sale and supply of those products; for their labelling and advertising; and for pharmacovigilance.

For the most part the Regulations implement Directive 2001/83/EC of the European Parliament and of the Council of 6 November 2001 on the community code relating to medicinal products for human use (as amended). They also provide for the enforcement in the United Kingdom of Regulation (EC) No 726/2004 laying down Community procedures for the authorisation and supervision of medicinal products for human and veterinary use and establishing a European Medicines Agency.

These Regulations consolidate the 1968 Medicines Act and its supporting regulations including:

- **The Medicines (Applications for Manufacturer's and Wholesale Dealer's Licences) Regulations 1971 (SI 1971 No. 974), as amended**

- Medicines (Manufacturer's Undertakings for Imported Products) Regulations 1977 (SI 1977 No. 1038), as amended
- Medicines for Human Use (Marketing Authorisations Etc.) Regulations 1994 (SI 1994 No. 3144), as amended
- Prescription Only Medicines (Human Use) Order 1997 (as amended) (SI 1997 No. 1830), as amended

The Medicines (Products for Human Use) (Fees) Regulations 2013 (2013 No. 532)

These Regulations make provision for the fees payable under the Medicines Act 1971 in respect of marketing authorizations, licences and certificates relating to medicinal products for human use.

The Medicines for Human Use (Clinical Trials) Regulations 2004 (SI 2004 No. 1031) as amended

These Regulations implement Directive 2001/20/EC on the approximation of laws, regulations and administrative provisions of the Member States relating to the implementation of good clinical practice in the conduct of clinical trials on medicinal products for human use.

The Unlicensed Medicinal Products for Human Use (Transmissible Spongiform Encephalopathies) (Safety) Regulations 2003 (SI 2003 No. 1680)

Regulates the importation and marketing of unlicensed medicinal products for human use in order to minimise the risk of the transmission of Transmissible Spongiform Encephalopathies via those products.

MHRA

MHRA: Licensing, Inspection and Enforcement for Human Medicines

Contents

Overview of the Medicines and Healthcare Products Regulatory Agency Group

In 2002, Ministers announced that the Medicines Control Agency and the Medical Devices Agency would be merged to form the Medicines and Healthcare products Regulatory Agency (MHRA). MHRA is responsible for regulating all medicines and medical devices in the UK by ensuring they work and are acceptably safe.

On the 1 April 2013 the National Institute for Biological Standards and Control (NIBSC), previously part of the Health Protection Agency (HPA), became a new centre of the Medicines and Healthcare Products Regulatory Agency Group alongside the Clinical Practice Research Datalink (CPRD).

MHRA and NIBSC have worked closely together for many years and have common interests in managing risks associated with biological medicines, facilitating development of new medicines safely and effectively, and maintaining UK expertise and ability to contribute to assuring the quality and safety of medicines in Europe and beyond.

These developments have created a new organisation that is a world leader in supporting science and research and the regulation of medicines and medical devices, strengthening the support provided to the UK's medicine's industry. The new Medicines and Healthcare Products Regulatory Agency group consists of:

- **MHRA Regulatory,** who protect health and improve lives by ensuring that medicines and medical devices work, and are acceptably safe; focusing on the core activities of product licensing, inspection and enforcement, and pharmacovigilance.
- **The Clinical Practice Research Datalink** (CPRD), which gives access to an unparalleled resource for conducting observational research and improving the efficiency of interventional research, across all areas of health, medicines and devices. CPRD joined the MHRA in 2012.
- **The National Institute for Biological Standards and Control,** world leaders in assuring the quality of biological medicines through product testing, developing standards and reference materials and carrying out applied research.

Medicines and Healthcare Products Regulatory Agency

MHRA	National Institute for Biological Standards Board (NIBSC)	Clinical Practice Research Datalink (CPRD)
• Operating a system of licensing, classification, monitoring (post-marketing surveillance) and enforcement for medicines.	• Devising and drawing up standards for the purity and potency of biological substances and designing appropriate test procedures.	• Managing and designing CPRD services to maximise the way anonymised NHS clinical data can be linked to enables many types of observational research and deliver research outputs that are beneficial to improving and safeguarding public health.
• Discharging statutory obligations for medical devices, including designating and monitoring the performance of notified bodies.	• Preparing, approving, holding and distributing standard preparations of biological substances.	
• Ensuring statutory compliance in medicines clinical trials and assessing medical device clinical trials proposals.	• Providing, or arranging for, the provision of laboratory testing facilities for the testing of biological substances, carrying out such testing, examining records of manufacture and quality control and reporting on the results.	
• Promulgating good practice in the safe use of medicines and medical devices.		
• Regulating the safety and quality of blood and blood components.	• Carrying out or arranging for the carrying out of research in connection with biological standards and control functions.	
• Discharging the functions of the UK Good Laboratory Practice Monitoring Authority (GLPMA).		
• Managing the activities of the British Pharmacopoeia (BP).		

Overview of MHRA

All licensed human medicines available in the UK are subject to rigorous scrutiny by MHRA before they can be used by patients. This ensures that human medicines meet acceptable standards on safety, quality and efficacy. It is the responsibility of MHRA and the expert advisory bodies set up by the Human Medicines Regulations 2012 [SI 2012/1916] (previously under the 1968 Medicines Act) to ensure that the sometimes difficult balance between safety and effectiveness is achieved. MHRA experts assess all applications for new human medicines to ensure they meet the required standards. This is followed up by a system of inspection and testing which continues throughout the lifetime of the medicine.

As the UK government's public health body which brings together the regulation of human medicines and medical devices, science and research the roles of MHRA are to:

- license medicines, manufacturers and distributors;
- register brokers of finished medicines and manufacturers, importers and distributors of active substances;
- regulate medical devices;
- approve UK clinical trials;
- monitor medicines and medical devices after licensing;
- ensure the safety and quality of blood;
- tackle illegal activity involving medicines, medical devices and blood;
- promote an understanding of the benefits and risks;
- facilitate the development of new medicines;
- support innovation in medicines and medical devices;
- be a leading provider of data and data services for healthcare research;
- work with international partners on issues; and
- provide a national voice for the benefits and risks of medicines, medical devices and medical technologies.

MHRA also hosts and supports a number of expert advisory bodies, including the Commission on Human Medicines (which replaced the Committee on the Safety of Medicines in 2005), and the British Pharmacopoeia Commission. In addition, as part of the European system of medicines approval, MHRA or other national bodies may be the Rapporteur or Co-rapporteur for any given pharmaceutical application, taking on the bulk of the verification work on behalf of all members, while the documents are still sent to other members as and where requested.

MHRA Innovation Office

One of the key objectives of MHRA is to support greater access to safe and effective medicinal products and medical devices. The timely introduction of innovative products benefits both patients and the public. This section provides information about MHRA's Innovation Office and highlights how you can get scientific and regulatory advice to support the development of innovational products.

MHRA's Innovation Office helps organisations that are developing innovative medicines, medical devices or using novel manufacturing processes to navigate the regulatory processes in order to be able to progress their products or technologies. Examples of innovative products include Advanced Therapy Medicinal Products (ATMPs), nanotechnology, stratified medicines, novel drug/device combinations and advanced manufacturing.

If you are a pharmaceutical researcher, developer, manufacturer, etc. and you have a question about an innovative medicine, device or novel manufacturing process, contact the MHRA Innovation Office using one of the routes below.

After contacting the office you will receive a response within 20 working days. Depending on the nature of the query, your response will consist of either a simple answer or a recommended course of action, which may involve regulatory or scientific advice.

SCIENTIFIC AND REGULATORY ADVICE

MHRA offers regulatory and scientific advice. For medicines, we currently carry out over 250 scientific advice meetings a year. Joint meetings can be held with the National Institute for Health and Care Excellence (NICE) to consider health technology assessment issues at the same time.

SCIENTIFIC ADVICE FROM THE EU

The European Medicines Agency (EMA) offers a comprehensive scientific advice service, available to provide assistance during the initial development of a medicine and during the post-authorisation phase. The advice is provided by the EMA's Committee for Medicinal Products for Human Use (CHMP),[1] based on recommendations of the Scientific Advice Working Party (SAWP).[2] Further advice on accessing scientific advice can be obtained from the EMA.[3]

---

[1] http://www.ema.europa.eu/ema/index.jsp?curl=pages/about_us/general/general_content_000094.jsp&mid=WC0b01ac0580028c79

[2] http://www.ema.europa.eu/ema/index.jsp?curl=pages/contacts/CHMP/people_listing_000022.jsp&mid=WC0b01ac0580028d94

[3] http://www.ema.europa.eu/ema/index.jsp?curl=pages/regulation/general/general_content_000049.jsp&mid=WC0b01ac05800229b9&jsenabled=true

SCIENTIFIC ADVICE FROM THE UK

MHRA offers a comprehensive scientific advice service which can assist companies in making decisions about a range of scientific and regulatory issues. Scientific advice can be requested at any stage of the initial development of a medicine and also during the pre-submission period. Please see MHRA webpages on 'Scientific Advice'.[4]

MHRA supporting innovation in medicines

MHRA supports innovation through:

Medicines

- membership on European committees (Commission on Human Medicinal Products (CHMP), CAT, COMP, PDCO) and CHMP Working Parties;[5]
- membership of European Good Distribution Practice (GDP)/Good Manufacturing Practice (GMP) Inspectors Working Group;
- advice given to EMA Innovation Task Force on a wide range of innovative technologies and products;
- working within the ICH network;
- writing regulatory and scientific guidance documents via the ICH and CHMP; and
- membership of European GDP/GMP Inspectors Working Group

Devices sector

- membership of European committees such as the Medical Devices Expert group (MDEG), Borderlines and Classification Group, New and Emerging Technologies Working Group (NET); and
- part of the International Medical Device Regulators Forum.

Inspection, Enforcement and Standards Division

MHRA's Inspection, Enforcement and Standards Division is responsible for ensuring compliance with the regulations and standards that apply to the manufacture, control and supply of medicines on the UK market.

---

[4] http://www.mhra.gov.uk/Howweregulate/Medicines/Licensingofmedicines/Informationforlicenceapplicants/Otherusefulservicesandinformation/Scientificadviceforlicenceapplicants/index.htm

[5] http://www.ema.europa.eu/ema/index.jsp?curl=pages/about_us/general/general_content_000217.jsp&mid=

Inspectorate

The Inspectorate Group in MHRA's Inspection, Enforcement and Standards Division is comprised of dedicated units for Good Manufacturing Practice (GMP), Good Distribution Practice (GDP), Good Laboratory Practice (GLP), Good Clinical Practice (GCP) and Good Pharmacovigilance Practice (GPvP).

Good Manufacturing Practice (GMP)

GMP Inspectors conduct inspections of pharmaceutical manufacturers and other organisations to assess compliance with EC guidance on Good Manufacturing Practice (GMP) and the relevant details contained in marketing authorisations and Clinical Trials Authorisations. They ensure that medicines supplied in the UK and wider EU meet consistent high standards of quality, safety and efficacy. Overseas manufacturing sites to be named on UK or EU marketing authorisations are also required to pass an inspection prior to approval of the marketing authorisation application. Following approval, a risk-based inspection programme maintains on-going surveillance of UK and overseas manufacturing site compliance with EC GMP.

GMP Inspectors are responsible for inspecting and authorising a range of manufacturers of sterile and non-sterile dosage forms, biological products, investigational medicinal products, herbal products and active pharmaceutical ingredients, in addition to certain analytical laboratories. The manufacture of unlicensed medicines by holders of Manufacturer "Specials" Licences in the UK NHS and commercial sector is also inspected on a routine basis to assess compliance with relevant legislation and GMP.

The safety and quality of human blood for transfusion, or for further manufacture into blood-derived medicines, is ensured through inspections of relevant collection, processing, testing and storage activities at Blood Establishments and UK Hospital Blood Banks. These inspections assess compliance with specific UK and EU regulatory requirements, which take into account the detailed principles of GMP.

GMP Inspectors serve on a number of UK, EU and international technical and standards committees and provide help and advice to senior managers, Ministers and colleagues across the Agency, as necessary. Support and expertise is also provided to the inspection programmes of the European Medicines Agency (EMA), European Directorate for Quality of Medicines (EDQM), and the World Health Organization (WHO).

Good Distribution Practice (GDP)

GDP Inspectors conduct inspections of sites of wholesale dealers to assess compliance with EU Guidelines on Good Distribution Practice (GDP) and the conditions of a wholesale dealer's licence.

Inspectors will ensure that medicinal products are handled, stored and transported under conditions as prescribed by the marketing authorisation or product specification.

Inspections are undertaken of new applicants and then subsequently on a routine schedule based on a risk assessment of the site.

There are a number of developments that had an impact on GDP during 2013 and going forward including:

- the Human Medicines Regulations 2012 [SI 2012/1916] which came into force in August 2012, replacing the majority of the Medicines Act 1968 and its supporting legislation;
- the transposition of the Falsified Medicines Directive 2011/62/EU into UK medicines legislation which extends GDP to any person or entity who procures, stores or supplies medicinal products, for export to countries outside of the EEA and to brokers of finished medicines within the EEA.
- the application of the revised EU Guidelines on GDP of the 5 November, which entered into force on 24 November 2013. This version replaced the earlier version, which entered into force on 8 September 2013, and introduced the following changes:
  - the maintenance of a quality system setting out responsibilities, processes and risk management principles in relation to wholesale activities;
  - suitable documentation which prevents errors from spoken communication;
  - sufficient competent personnel to carry out all the tasks for which the wholesale distributor is responsible;
  - adequate premises, installations and equipment so as to ensure proper storage and distribution of medicinal products;
  - appropriate management of complaints, returns, suspected falsified medicinal products and recalls;
  - outsourced activities correctly defined to avoid misunderstandings;
  - rules for transport in particular to protect medicinal products against breakage, adulteration and theft, and to ensure that temperature conditions are maintained within acceptable limits during transport;
  - specific rules for brokers (person involved in activities in relation to the sale or purchase of medicinal products, except for wholesale distribution, that do not include physical handling the products).

The revised EU Guidelines on GDP have been included in this publication.

Good Laboratory Practice (GLP)

GLP Inspectors conduct inspections of UK facilities that carry out non-clinical studies for submission to domestic and international regulatory authorities to assess the safety of new chemicals to humans, animals and the environment. These inspections are designed to assure that studies are performed in accordance with the relevant EC directives and the Organisation for Economic Co-operation and Development (OECD) principles as required by OECD Council acts relating to the Mutual Acceptance of Data. The range of test facilities to be monitored include those involved in the testing of human and veterinary pharmaceuticals, agrochemicals, food and feed additives, industrial chemicals and cosmetics.

Good Clinical Practice (GCP)

The GCP Inspectorate is responsible for inspecting clinical trials for compliance with Good Clinical Practice (GCP). Compliance with this good practice provides assurance that the rights, safety and well-being of trial subjects are protected, and that the results of the clinical trials are credible and accurate.

The function of the GCP Inspectorate is to assess the compliance of organisations with UK and EU legislation relating to the conduct of clinical trials in investigational medicinal products. This is achieved through carrying out inspections of sponsor organisations that hold Clinical Trial Authorisations (CTA), organisations that provide services to clinical trial sponsors or investigator sites.

Good Pharmacovigilance Practice (GPvP)

The Pharmacovigilance Inspectorate conducts inspections of the pharma-covigilance systems of marketing authorisation holders to assess compliance with the requirements of the UK and European legislation and guidelines relating to the monitoring of the safety of medicines given to patients.

The Data Processing Group

The Data Processing Group was formed in 2011 by consolidating the existing Process Licensing, Export Certificates, Import Notifications and Defective Medicines Reporting Centre functions to reside in a single Business Unit as part of the Inspection, Enforcement and Standards Division.

Manufacturer's and wholesale dealer's licence/authorisations

Manufacture of and wholesale dealing in medicinal products are licensable activities under UK and EU legislation. These licences are referred to as process licences and include a wide range of licences covering diverse activities listed below:

- Licences for the manufacture/importation of licensed medicinal products for human use, commonly abbreviated to MIA.
- "Specials" licences for the manufacture/importation of unlicensed medicinal products for human use, commonly abbreviated to MS.
- Authorisations for the manufacture/importation of Investigational Medicinal Products for human use, commonly abbreviated to MIA (IMP).
- Authorisations for the manufacture/importation of licensed medicinal products for veterinary use, commonly abbreviated to ManA.
- "Specials" licences for the manufacture of unlicensed medicinal products for veterinary use, commonly abbreviated to ManSA.
- Authorisation for the manufacture of Exempt Advanced Therapy Medicinal Products, commonly abbreviated to MeAT.
- Licences for the wholesale dealing of medicinal products for human use, commonly abbreviated to WDA(H) (including those covering unlicensed medicines obtained from another EEA Member State).
- Licences for the wholesale dealing/importation of medicinal products for veterinary use, commonly abbreviated to WDA(V).
- Blood Establishment Authorisations, commonly abbreviated to BEA.

The Data Processing team process all applications for new licences, variations to existing licences, changes of ownership, terminations, cancellations as well as suspensions and revocations on the instructions of the Inspection Action Group (IAG), making extensive use of computer technology to do so. They are also responsible for issuing Certificates of Good Manufacturing Practice (GMP) and Good Distribution Practice (GDP) on behalf of the GMP and GDP Inspectorate.

Registrations

The Falsified Medicines Directive 2011/62/EU made it a requirement that certain activities require registration and that a minimum of information be published on a publically accessible registers. These activities include:

- Brokering of finished human medicines.
- Manufacture, importation and distribution of active substances.

The Data Processing team process all applications for registration, variations to existing registrations, annual compliance reports, terminations, cancellations, suspensions and revocations making extensive use of computer technology to do so.

Export Certificates

The Data Processing team are also responsible for issuing certificates in support of the World Health Organization (WHO) scheme on the quality of pharmaceutical products moving in international commerce (often referred to as export certificates):

- Certificate of a pharmaceutical product (CPP). This certificate complies with the WHO format.
- Certificate of licensing status (CLS). This certificate complies with the WHO format.
- Certificate of manufacturing status (CMS).
- Certificate for the importation of a pharmaceutical constituent (CPC).
- Statement of licensing status of a pharmaceutical product(s).

Importing unlicensed medicines – import notifications

Under regulation 46 of the Human Medicines Regulations 2012 [SI 2012/1916] a medicine must have a marketing authorisation (includes Product Licences) unless exempt. One of these exemptions, which is in regulation 167 to these regulations, is for the supply of unlicensed medicinal products for the special needs of individual patients, commonly, but incorrectly called "named patients". Prospective importers must hold a relevant licence and must notify MHRA of their intention to import:

- for import from within the European Economic Area (EEA), a Wholesale Dealer's Licence valid for import and handling unlicensed relevant medicinal products;
- for import from outside of the EEA, a Manufacturer's 'Specials' Licence valid for import.

The Data Processing team makes use of a bespoke computer system (INS) to enter the information, refer flagged requests to Pharmaceutical Assessors for assessment as required and issue confirmation letters authorising or rejecting importation.

Defective Medicines Report Centre (DMRC)

MHRA's Defective Medicines Report Centre (DMRC) plays a major part in the protection of public health by minimising the hazard to patients arising from the distribution of defective medicinal products. It does this by providing an emergency assessment and communications system between suppliers of medicinal products, the regulatory authorities and the users. It achieves this by receiving and assessing reports of suspected defective medicines, monitoring and as necessary advising and directing appropriate actions by the responsible authorisation holder and communicating the details of this action as necessary and with appropriate urgency to recipients of the products and other interested parties in the UK and elsewhere by means of drug alerts.

Manufacturers and importers are obliged to report to the licensing authority (MHRA) any quality defect in a medicinal product which could result in a recall or restriction on supply. Other users and distributors of medicinal products are encouraged to do this.

Where a defective medicine is considered to present a risk to public health, the marketing authorisation holder, or the manufacturer as appropriate, is responsible for recalling the affected batch(es) or, in extreme cases, removing all batches of the product from the market. The DMRC will normally support this action by the issue of a drug alert notification to healthcare professionals. Drug alerts are classed from 1 to 4 according to their criticality and the speed with which action must be taken to remove the defective medicine from the distribution chain and, where necessary, from the point of dispensing and use. This varies from immediate action for a Class 1 alert, to action within five days for a Class 3 alert. In some low-risk circumstances the product may be allowed to remain in the supply chain when the DMRC will issue a Class 4 "caution in use" alert.

The DMRC is also part of the European Rapid Alert System, and in the case of Class 1 and Class 2 will notify regulators in other countries using the European Rapid Alert System.

Enforcement Group

Medicines legislation contains statutory provisions to enforce the requirements of the Human Medicines Regulations 2012 [SI 2012/1916] and the remaining provisions of the 1968 Medicines Act.

This enforcement role is carried out by MHRA's Enforcement Group which is comprised of a Case Referrals Team, Intelligence Analysts, Investigations Team, Prosecution Unit and Policy/Relationships management.

The legislation confers certain powers, including rights of entry, powers of inspection, seizure, sampling and production of documents. Duly authorised Investigation Officers investigate cases using these powers and, where appropriate, criminal prosecutions are brought by the Crown Prosecution Service (CPS). MHRA investigators also investigate offences under other legislation such as the Fraud Act, Trademarks Act and the Offences Against the Person Act.

All reported breaches of medicines legislation are investigated. Reports are processed and risk-assessed before a course of action is agreed in line with our published Enforcement Strategy.

The aim of the Intelligence Unit is to drive forward the implementation of intelligence-led enforcement and enable a more proactive approach to the acquisition and development of information. The Unit acts as a co-ordination point for all information-gathering activities and works in conjunction with a wide network of public and professional bodies and trade associations, e.g. UK Border Force, UK Border Agency, Department of Health, Trading Standards and Port Health Authorities, the Police Service; and professional organisations such as the General Pharmaceutical Council (GPhC), General Medical Council and the Association of the British Pharmaceutical Industry (ABPI). Additionally, there is a network of other regulatory agencies and law enforcement bodies within the European Community and in other countries through which the Enforcement Group can exchange information and follow trends in pharmaceutical crime.

The Enforcement Group monitors trends in pharmaceutical crime and co-ordinates initiatives to counteract criminal activity. In particular, the availability of counterfeit medicines is a key priority area and an anti-counterfeiting strategy has been agreed and implemented.

Compliance Management and Inspection Action Group

Compliance Escalation process

Compliance Escalation is a non-statutory process to take action in response to poor compliance which does not yet meet the threshold for consideration of adverse regulatory action. Compliance Escalation is managed via the Compliance Management Team (CMT); a non-statutory group of senior GMDP inspectors who coordinate and advise on compliance management activities arising from chronic or significant GMP deficiencies. The main aim of the Compliance Escalation process is to direct companies towards a state of compliance, thus avoiding the need for regulatory action and the potential adverse impact to patient health through lack of availability of medicines as a result of action against an authorisation, as well as avoiding reputational and commercial damage for the manufacturer and product owner.

The specific inspection case issues are considered by CMT, who make decisions in conjunction with the inspector regarding the proportionate inspection and non-inspection compliance management actions required. This may include making recommendations on close monitoring of compliance improvement work through inspection, requested meetings with company senior management, and correspondence with company senior management, alerting them to the compliance concerns, and clearly outlining the consequences of continued non-compliance.

Decisions on compliance management actions are communicated to the company, following consideration of any written responses to a post-inspection letter if relevant. The site inspector(s) and CMT will continue to monitor the effectiveness of these actions. The CMT process may also be initiated by the Inspection Action Group (IAG) following referral for significant or serious GMP deficiencies. In cases where consideration of adverse licensing action is no longer required due to improvements or mitigating actions, IAG may close their case referral and request that CMT maintain compliance management oversight until completion of the remediation plans. Upon satisfactory conclusion of the remediation work, the company will be returned to the routine risk-based inspection programme; however, referral for consideration of regulatory action may still occur if the required improvements are not achieved in a timely manner.

Referral to Inspection Action Group

Critical findings are routinely referred to MHRA's Inspection Action Group (IAG). The group considers referrals involving serious/critical GMP deficiencies. The primary objective of IAG is to protect public health by ensuring that licensable activities in the manufacturing and distribution of medicinal products meet the required regulatory standards.

The IAG is a non-statutory, multi-disciplinary group constituted to advise the Director of Inspection, Enforcement and Standards Division (IE&S) on any recommendation for regulatory or adverse licensing action appropriate to the Division. There are two distinct groups:

- IAG1 considers issues related to GMP, GDP and Blood Establishment Authorisations (GMP/GDP/BEA) and has 24 scheduled meetings per year, normally the first and third Tuesdays of each month; and
- IAG2 considers issues related to Good Clinical and Good Pharmaco-vigilance Practices (GCP/GPvP) and has 12 scheduled meetings per year, normally the fourth Tuesday of each month.

There may be occasions when there is not enough business to make a meeting worth while. Conversely, there have been several occasions where an urgent issue has arisen, and an emergency meeting called.

The following attend both IAG1 and IAG2:

- the regulatory unit manager or deputy (chair);
- at least one medical assessor from MHRA Licensing Division;
- at least one pharmaceutical assessor from MHRA Licensing Division;
- a solicitor from Government Legal Services;

- at least one member of the IAG Secretariat;
- any inspector making a referral to the IAG;
- a representative from Enforcement Operations (if required); and
- members of MHRA staff may also attend for training purposes.

In addition, the following will attend IAG1:

- an expert/senior GMP inspector;
- an expert/senior GDP inspector;
- if required a representative from the Veterinary Medicines Directorate (external link); and
- an expert in blood and blood products (if required).

In addition, the following will attend IAG2:

- an expert/senior GCP inspector;
- an expert/senior GPvP inspector;
- the Clinical Trials Unit manager or deputy; and
- the Pharmacovigilance Risk Management Group manager or deputy.

REASONS FOR REFERRAL

This will usually happen if, during the inspection process, the inspector has identified one or more critical "deficiencies" as a result of a Good Practice Standards (GxP) inspection. However, a referral may also be made as a result of a licence variation, the failure to contact an organisation, the refusal of an organisation to accept an inspection, the outcome of enforcement activity, the outcome of a product recall or from an issue raised by another Member State.

The company will be informed during the closing meeting of an inspection that a referral to IAG will be made. This will be further confirmed in the post-inspection letter. From that point, correspondence between the company and the Agency should go via the IAG Secretariat.

How the process works:

(1) Inspection reveals serious (critical) deficiencies and informs company of IAG referral.
(2) Post-inspection letter is issued to company signed by responsible operations manager/lead inspector.
(3) IAG discusses the case at its next available meeting (if necessary an emergency meeting can be called).
(4) IAG proposes its action to the divisional director for approval.
(5) The referred company is informed of IAG action and next steps.
(6) Actions are followed up at subsequent meetings until the situation is resolved.
(7) The matter is kept on the agenda until IAG is satisfied that the referral can be closed.

IAG POSSIBLE ACTIONS

IAG1 (GMP/GDP/BEA)

- refusal to grant a licence or a variation;
- proposal to suspend the licence for a stated period;
- notification of immediate suspension of the licence for a stated period (no longer than three months);
- proposal to revoke the licence;
- action to remove a Qualified Person/Responsible Person (QP/RP) from the licence;
- issue a Cease and Desist order in relation to a Blood Establishment Authorisation;
- issue a warning letter to the company/individual;
- request a written justification for actions of a QP/RP;
- referral of a QP to his/her professional body;
- increased inspection frequency;
- request the company/individual attend a meeting at the Agency; or
- refer to the Enforcement Group for further consideration.

IAG2 (GCP/GPvP)

- issue an infringement notice in relation to a clinical trial;
- suspend or revoke a clinical trial authorisation;
- further follow-up inspections, or triggered inspections at related organisations (e.g. issues in GCP may trigger a GMP inspection);
- referral to CHMP (Committee for Medicinal Products for Human Use) for consideration for against a marketing authorisation (eg suspended, varied or revoked);
- liaison and coordinated action with EMA (European Medicines Agency) and other Member States regarding concerns;
- refer the case to the EMA for consideration of the use of the EU Infringement Regulation (which could result in a fine);
- request a written justification for action of a QPPV (Qualified Person responsible for pharmacovigilance);
- request the company/individual attend a meeting at the Agency; or
- refer to the Enforcement Group for further consideration.

In the case of inspections in third countries:

- a refusal to name a site on a marketing authorisation;
- a recommendation that a site be removed from a marketing authorisation;
- the issuing of a GMP non-compliance statement;
- in the case of an adverse (voluntary or triggered) active pharmaceutical ingredients (API) inspection, this could result in the removal of the API site from the marketing authorisation; or

- in the case of an adverse (voluntary or triggered) investigational medicinal products (IMP) inspection, this could result in the suspension of a clinical trial.

In all cases, an action could result in the withdrawal of product (API, IMP medicinal product, etc.) from the market. This specific action is, however, handled by the Defective Medicines Reporting Centre (DMRC) rather than directly by IAG.

LEGAL BASIS FOR THIS ACTION

The legal basis for licensing action is contained in:

- The Human Medicines Regulations 2012;
- The Medicines for Human Use (Clinical Trials) Regulations 2004; and
- The Blood Safety and Quality Regulations 2005.

WHAT A LICENCE HOLDER SHOULD DO IF REFERRED TO IAG

In the first instance, a referral should be treated as a requirement to immediately correct the deficiencies identified during the inspection and report completed actions to the IAG Secretariat/Inspectorate as soon as possible.

If the referral results in an immediate suspension of a manufacturing/wholesale dealer's licence, there are no rights of appeal for the immediate suspension (which can last no longer than three months). During this time a company should be focused on correcting the inspection deficiencies.

If the referral results in a proposed suspension, variation or revocation of a licence a company will have the following appeal options prior to a decision being made:

- may make written representations to the licensing authority (MHRA); or
- may appear before and be heard by a person appointed for the purpose by the licensing authority (a fee of £10,000 will be charged for a person appointed request).

If a company submits written representations, the licensing authority shall take those representations into account before determining the matter. In practice, this means that any proposed action will not be progressed until the written representations have been reviewed and considered by IAG and a recommendation made to the Divisional Director on whether to proceed with the action or not.

If a company submits a request for a Person Appointed Hearing, this will be taken forward by the Panel Secretariat, which sits within the MHRA's Policy Division. Any proposed action will not be progressed until the Person Appointed Hearing has taken place.

It should be noted that a Person Appointed Hearing will only offer its opinion into whether a licence condition has been contravened. A final decision on whether to suspend or revoke a licence will still rest with the licensing authority, who will take the report of the Person Appointed Hearing into account.

Follow up actions that may be taken:

- a re-inspection to ensure corrective actions implemented;
- request for regular updates on the corrective action plan;
- the issue of a short dated GMP certificate;
- recommended increase of inspection frequency;
- continued monitoring of the company by IAG via inspectorate updates; or
- if serious and persistent non-compliance continues referral for consideration of criminal prosecution.

Contact for further information: IAGSecretariat@mhra.gsi.gov.uk

Advice

MHRA publishes a series of Guidance Notes relating to its statutory functions. Those of particular interest to manufacturers and wholesale dealers include:

GN 5   Notes for applicants and holders of a manufacturer's licence
GN 6   Notes for applicants and holders of a wholesale dealer's licence (WDA(H)) or broker registration
GN 8   A guide to what is a medicinal product
GN 14   The supply of unlicensed medicinal products "Specials"

These Guidance Notes and a list of others available may be obtained from MHRA's website or from MHRA's Customer Services Team.

Contact details are as follows:

Address:
Customer Services, MHRA, 151 Buckingham Palace Road, Victoria, London SW1W 9SZ, UK
Telephone: +44 (0)20 3080 6000 (weekdays 0900–1700)
Fax: +44 (0)20 3118 9803
E-mail: info@mhra.gsi.gov.uk
Website: www.mhra.gov.uk

UK Guidance on the Manufacture, Importation and Distribution of Active Substances

Contents

Introduction

EU Directive 2001/83/EC lays down the rules for the manufacture, import, marketing and supply of medicinal products and ensures the functioning of the internal market for medicinal products while safeguarding a high level of protection of public health in the EU.

The falsification of medicinal products is a global problem, requiring effective and enhanced international coordination and cooperation in order to ensure that anti-falsification strategies are more effective, in particular as regards sale of such products via the Internet. To that end, the Commission and Member States are cooperating closely and supporting ongoing work in international fora on this subject, such as the Council of Europe, Europol and the United Nations. In addition, the Commission, working closely with Member States, is cooperating with the competent authorities of third countries with a view to effectively combating the trade in falsified medicinal products at a global level.

Active substances are those substances which give a medicinal product its therapeutic effect. They are the Active Pharmaceutical Ingredient (API).

Falsified active substances and active substances that do not comply with applicable requirements of Directive 2001/83/EC pose serious risks to public health.

The Falsified Medicines Directive 2011/62/EU amends Directive 2001/83/EC in order to facilitate the enforcement of and control of compliance with Union rules relating to active substances. It makes a number of significant changes to the controls on active substances intended for use in the manufacture of a medicinal product for human use.

A number of new terms have been introduced into the 2001 Directive by the Falsified Medicines Directive, including "falsified medicinal product" and "active substance". The aim of this is to ensure that other amendments introduced by the Falsified Medicines Directive are consistently interpreted and applied across the EU.

The 2001 Directive has been amended to permit the European Commission to adopt the following:

- the principles and guidelines of good manufacturing practice for active substances, by means of a delegated act; and
- the principles of good distribution practice for active substances, by means of adopted guidelines.

Registration

To provide a greater level of control, and transparency of supply, for active substances within the European Community manufacturers, importers and distributors of active substances have to notify the relevant competent authorities of their activities and provide certain details. In the UK this will be MHRA. The competent authority has an obligation to enter these details into a Community Database (EudraGMDP) following the determination of a successful application for registration. The competent authority may then conduct inspections against the requirements of the relevant good practices before permitting such businesses to start trading. Manufacturers, importers and distributors of active substances will not only be subject to inspection on the basis of suspicions of non-compliance, but also on the basis of risk-analysis.

Authorised manufacturers of medicinal products who also manufacture and/or import active substances, either for use in their own products or products manufactured by other companies, are not exempt from the requirement to register.

Persons who are requested to import an active substance from a non-EEA country that provide facilities solely for transporting the active substance, or where they are acting as an import agent, imports the active substance solely to the order of another person who holds a certificate of good manufacturing practice issued by the licensing authority, are not required to register.

The registration regime for manufacturers, importers and distributors of active substances will be subject to an application procedure, followed by a determination procedure completed by MHRA.

The person applying for registration must notify MHRA immediately of any changes which have taken place as regards to the information in the registration form, where such changes may have an impact on quality or safety of the active substances that are manufactured, imported or distributed. These changes shall be treated as incorporated in the application form.

MHRA must grant or refuse an application for registration within 60 working days beginning immediately after the day on which a valid application is received.

MHRA will notify the applicant within 60 days of receipt of a valid application for registration whether they intend to undertake an inspection.

The applicant may not undertake any activity before either:

- 60 days have elapsed and the applicant has not been notified of the Agency's intention to inspect, or
- following inspection the Agency has notified the applicant that they may commence their activities.

After inspection MHRA will prepare a report and communicate that report to the applicant. The applicant will have the opportunity to respond to the report. Within 90 days of an inspection MHRA shall issue an appropriate good practice certificate to the applicant, indicating that the applicant complies with the requirements of the relevant good practices. Where an applicant is found to be non-compliant with the requisite standards, a statement of non-compliance will be issued by MHRA.

If after 60 days of the receipt of the application form MHRA has not notified the applicant of their intention to carry out an inspection, the applicant may commence their business activity and regard themselves as registered. MHRA will issue a certificate to the applicant and enter the details into the Community Database.

This Community Database which is publicly available will enable competent authorities in other EEA Member States or other legal entities, to establish the bona fides and compliance of manufacturers, importers and distributors of active substances established in the UK and those in other EEA territories. MHRA will investigate concerns with regards to UK registrations of non-compliance and reciprocal arrangements will apply with other EEA Member States.

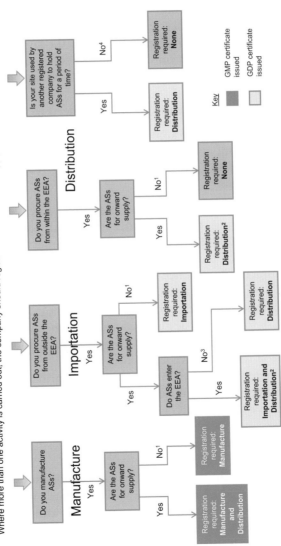

MHRA

Registration requirements for UK companies involved in the sourcing and supply of active substances (ASs) to be used in the manufacture of licensed human medicines.

This flowchart may be used to determine the appropriate registration required for UK companies. Where more than one activity is carried out, the company should register for all activities that apply.

Do you manufacture ASs?

Manufacture

Yes → **Are the ASs for onward supply?**
- Yes → Registration required: **Manufacture and Distribution**
- No[1] → Registration required: **Manufacture**

Do you procure ASs from outside the EEA?

Importation

Yes → **Are the ASs for onward supply?**
- Yes → **Do ASs enter the EEA?**
  - Yes → Registration required: **Importation and Distribution[2]**
  - No[3] → Registration required: **Distribution**
- No[1] → Registration required: **Importation**

Do you procure ASs from within the EEA?

Distribution

Yes → **Are the ASs for onward supply?**
- Yes → Registration required: **Distribution[2]**
- No[1] → Registration required: **None**

Is your site used by another registered company to hold ASs for a period of time?
- Yes → Registration required: **Distribution**
- No[4] → Registration required: **None**

Key
- ▓ GMP certificate issued
- ░ GDP certificate issued

1. Site holds a manufacturer's licence and uses the ASs in the manufacture of the finished dose form.
2. Where the registration holder contracts out the physical handling of the AS, the company that physically handles the product should be named as a 3rd party site on the registration if they hold the ASs and this takes place in the UK. In addition, the company should hold its own registration. If the company are based in another EEA State, they should be registered with the competent authority in that State.
3. ASs procured from outside the EEA are supplied directly to customers based outside the EEA.
4. ASs are not held (stored) for any length of time and the company are simply contracted to transport the ASs.

Figure 4.1 Registration requirements for UK companies involved in the sourcing and supply of active substances (ASs) to be used in the manufacture of licensed human medicines.

Conditions of Registration as a Manufacturer, Importer or Distributor of an Active Substance

A person in the UK may not import, manufacture or distribute, an active substance for use in a licensed human medicine unless they are registered with MHRA in accordance with the Human Medicines Regulations 2012 and the respective conditions of those Regulations are met.

Registration holders must submit to MHRA an annual update of any changes to the information provided in the application. Any changes which may have an impact on the quality or safety of the active substance which the registrant is permitted to handle must be notified to the Agency immediately.

An annual compliance report will need to be submitted:

- in relation to any application made before 31 March 2013, the date of application; and
- in relation to each subsequent reporting year, 30 April following the end of that year.

Where the Commission has adopted principles and guidelines of good manufacturing practice under the third paragraph of Article 47[1] of Directive 2001/83/EC which applies to an active substance manufactured in the UK, the registered manufacturer must comply with good manufacturing practice in relation to that active substance.

Where the Commission has adopted principles and guidelines of good distribution practice under the fourth paragraph of Article 47 of Directive 2001/83/EC which applies to an active substance distributed in the UK, the registered distributor must comply with good distribution practice in relation to that active substance.

Where the Commission has adopted principles and guidelines of good manufacturing practice under the third paragraph of Article 47 of Directive 2001/83/EC which applies to an active substance imported into the UK and where an active substance is imported from a third country the registered importer must comply with good distribution practice in relation to the active substance.

Under such circumstances the active substances must have been manufactured in accordance with standards which are at least equivalent to EU good manufacturing practice and when imported must be accompanied by a written confirmation from the competent authority of the exporting third country unless a waiver exists.

---

[1] Article 47 was amended by Directive 2011/62/EU of the European Parliament and of the Council (OJ No L 174, 1.7.2011, p. 74).

GMP for Active Substances

Directive 2001/83/EC has been amended to include a new definition of "active substance" which means any substance or mixture of substances intended to be used in the manufacture of a medicinal product and that, when used in its production, becomes an active ingredient of that product intended to exert a pharmacological, immunological or metabolic action with a view to restoring, correcting or modifying physiological functions or to make a medical diagnosis.

The manufacture of active substances should be subject to good manufacturing practice regardless of whether those active substances are manufactured in the Union or imported. Where active substances are manufactured in third countries it should be ensured that such substances have been manufactured to the relevant European standards of good manufacturing practice (GMP), so as to provide a level of protection of public health equivalent to that provided for by EU law.

A manufacturer or assembler of an active substance will have to comply with the principles and guidelines for GMP for active substances. Manufacture, in relation to an active substance, includes any process carried out in the course of making the substance and the various processes of dividing up, packaging, and presentation of the active substance. Assemble, in relation to an active substance, includes the various processes of dividing up, packaging and presentation of the substance, and "assembly" has a corresponding meaning. These activities will be the subject of a GMP certificate.

Importers of an active substance from a third country have to comply with the guidelines for Good Distribution Practice (GDP) in relation to the active substance. This activity will be the subject of a GDP certificate.

Distributors of an active substance within the UK which has been sourced from a manufacturer or an importer within the EU will have to comply with the guidelines for GDP for active substances. This activity will be the subject of a GDP certificate.

The 2001 Directive has been amended to permit the European Commission to adopt the following:

- the principles and guidelines of good manufacturing practice for active substances, by means of a delegated act; and
- the principles of good distribution practice for active substances, by means of adopted guidelines.

GMP for active substances is contained in Part II of the EU guidelines on Good Manufacturing Practice.

GDP for Active Substances

In February 2013 the European Commission consulted on its draft "Guidelines on the principles of good distribution practices for active substances for medicinal products for human use".

The draft text sets out the quality system elements for the procuring, importing, holding, supplying or exporting active substances. However the scope of the proposed text excludes activities consisting of re-packaging, re-labelling or dividing up of active substances which are manufacturing activities and as such are subject to the guidelines on GMP of active substances. The draft text of the guidelines covers:

- Quality System
- Personnel
- Documentation
- Orders
- Procedures
- Records
- Premises and Equipment
- Receipt
- Storage
- Deliveries to Customers
- Transfer of Information
- Returns
- Complaints and Recalls
- Self-inspections.

Written Confirmation

The Falsified Medicines Directive modifies EU Medicines Directive 2001/83/EC and from 2 July 2013 introduces new requirements for active substances imported into the EEA for use in the manufacture of authorised medicinal products.

The Falsified Medicines Directive requires importers of active substances to obtain written confirmations from competent authorities in non-EEA countries ("third countries") that the standards of manufacture of active substances at manufacturing sites on their territory are equivalent to EU good manufacturing practice (EU GMP). These confirmations are required before importation of active substances into the EU.

Each shipment of active substance received should be accompanied by a written confirmation from the competent authority of the exporting third country, stating that the active substance has been:

- manufactured to GMP standards at least equivalent to those laid down in the European Union;
- the third country manufacturing plant is subject to regular, strict and transparent inspections, and effective enforcement of GMP;
- in the event of non-conformance of the manufacturing site on inspection, such findings will be communicated to the European Union without delay.

The template for the written confirmation has been published in Part III of EudraLex, Volume 4 and is included in Chapter 2 of the Orange Guide.

Waiver from Written Confirmation

The Falsified Medicines Directive provides two waivers if written confirmations are not provided. The first is where the regulatory framework applicable to active substances in those third countries has been assessed by the European Commission (EC) as providing an equivalent level of protection of public health over active substance manufacture and distribution to those applied in the EU. This assessment follows a request from the exporting third country's competent authority, and considers the regulatory framework for active substance manufacture and control and its equivalence to EU standards. Only if the exporting country is on the EC's ("white") list is the requirement for a written confirmation from that country's competent authority removed.

The second waiver is where the third country active substance manufacturing site has been inspected by an EU Member State, has issued a certificate of compliance with EU-GMP and that it remains within its period of validity. This is an exceptional waiver intended to apply where it is necessary to ensure the availability of medicinal products. Member States using this waiver should communicate this fact to the European Commission in accordance with the legislation (Article 46b(4)). MHRA has notified the European Commission of its intent to use this waiver should that be necessary.

Procedure for Active Substance Importation

A summary of the overall active substance import process has been developed to promote a common expectation and common approaches by Member States and is available on the Heads of Medicines Agencies, website: http://www.hma.eu/43.html. The flow chart is reproduced here:

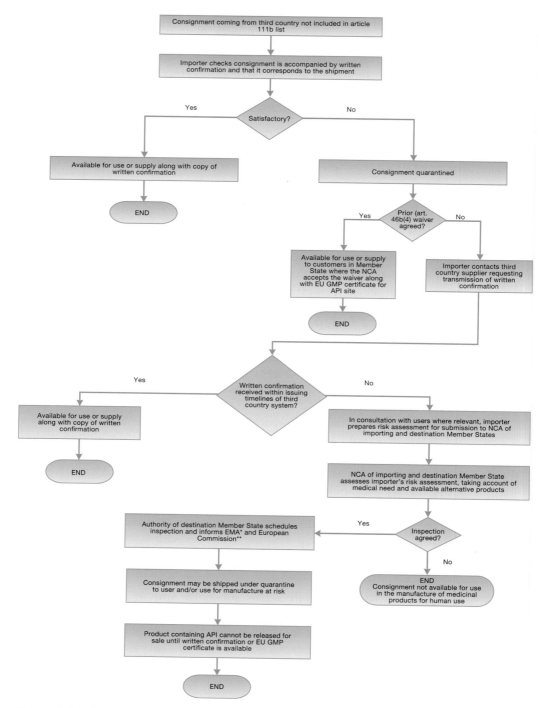

Figure 4.2 A flowchart of the overall active substance import process
*GMPINS@ema.europa.eu
**sanco-pharmaceuticals-d6@ec.europa.eu

Procedure for Waiver from Written Confirmation

UK based companies (registered importers and manufacturers who also import directly) who wish to import active substances under the second waiver should apply to gmpinspectorate@mhra.gsi.gov.uk using the form provided below which is available on the MHRA website.

Application Form for a waiver from the requirement to supply Written Confirmation with consignments of an imported Active Substance on the basis of a GMP certification of the Active Substance Manufacturer by an EEA Member State

A. Details of Third Country Manufacturing Site

Name of Active Substance : _____
(Note: Only one active substance permitted per Waiver application. Use INN nomenclature)

Name of Active Substance Manufacturer : _____
Address of Active Substance Manufacturer : _____
_____
_____

Country : _____
Third Country Competent Authority : _____
site / facility reference number (if known)

B. Reason for Application for this Waiver

The manufacturer / importer should attach a document explaining the reason for requesting this waiver. It should be noted that if the active substance is being sourced from a third country where the authority there is known to issue Written Confirmations then under normal circumstances it would be expected that a Written Confirmation would be the basis for importation of active substances from that country.

C. Details of GMP Certification

Any differences between the name and address supplied above and those details supplied on the GMP certificate must be justified in order to ensure efficient processing of the application.

Name of authority which issued the GMP certificate : _____
Inspection Date Referenced on GMP certificate : _____
Period of validity of GMP certificate* (if stated) : _____
(*this is 3 years unless there is a statement to the contrary)
Please attach a copy of the GMP certificate to this application form.

D. Details of Waiver Applicant

The Waiver Application may be submitted either by a site which has been registered with the MHRA for importation activities in the UK relating to active substances or by an authorised manufacturer / importer of human medicines in the UK which is using the imported active substance for manufacture of medicines for human use (excludes Investigational Medicinal Products) at its manufacturing address. If the importation activities (purchase of the active substance from a third country site or acting as the direct site of physical importation of the active substance) are being carried out directly by an authorised manufacturer of human medicines then both sections D1 and D2 below should be completed.

D1. Active Substance Importer

Active Substance Importers Registration No.:_____
Importation activity carried out for this active substance
(tick all that apply) ☐ Procurement (Purchasing) ☐ Site of physical importation
Registered Name of Importer :_____

Registered Address of Importer :_____

_____

_____

Country   UK

D2. Authorised Manufacturer of Human Medicines using Imported Active Substance

Manufacturer's / Importers Authorisation No. :_____

Name of Authorised Manufacturer   : _____

Manufacturing Site Address   : _____

_____

_____

Country   UK

E. Signature of Waiver Applicant

Signature   :_____ Date:_____

Name (Print) :_____

Position   :_____

F. Decision by MHRA on Waiver

Waiver Number:_____

Waiver approved (Yes / No):_____

Signature:_____ Date:_____

Name (Print):_____

Position :_____

National Contingency Guidance

MHRA acknowledges that the introduction of these additional require-ments may in some instance make the sourcing of active substances from some third countries difficult in the short term following 2 July 2013. MHRA has therefore developed contingency plans that would allow the Agency, in cases where there is an overriding need to ensure continued supply of specific active substances after 2 July 2013, to provide an opinion on the importation of the active substance to permit manufacture, QP certification and supply of finished medicinal products. The aim of these contingency plans is to ensure, as per the aims of the Falsified Medicines Directive, the continued supply of active substances of appropriate quality and maintain the responsibility for the quality of the authorised medicinal products with the manufacturer, as is the case under the current legislation in force. Where these supply difficulties exist, please contact the GMP inspectorate at GMPinspectorate@mhra.gsi.gov.uk.

Therefore for the short term only and where:

(a) the third country active substance manufacturing site is not covered by a written confirmation; and

(b) the exporting country has not been assessed by the EC as having standards equivalent to EU GMP; and

(c) the third country active substance manufacturing site is not the subject, following inspection, of a current certificate of compliance with EU GMP,

MHRA is actively seeking further information from impacted UK manufacturing sites identified through the active substance mapping exercise. Where UK Manufacturing Authorisation Holders ("MIA Holder") have determined that their third country active substance sources are at risk and have not been contacted by MHRA they should provide evidence in a submission / declaration template that:

(a) the active substance manufacturing site has been audited in the last three years either by himself or by a third party acting on his behalf and found to be operating in compliance with EU GMP for active substances; and

(b) the third country active substance manufacturing site is the subject, following inspection, of a current certificate of compliance with GMP issued by a recognised national authority or international organisation e.g. US-FDA, EU-MRA partners, EU-ACCA partners, PIC/S member states and the WHO.

UK based companies (registered importers and manufacturers who also import directly) who wish to import active substances under this guidance should apply to GMPinspectorate@mhra.gsi.gov.uk using the form provided at the end of this section which is available on the MHRA website.

Where the MIA Holder can make the first declaration but cannot declare that the third country active substance manufacturing site is the subject, following inspection, of a current certificate of compliance with GMP issued by a recognised national authority or international organisation then MHRA intends to enter details of the third country active substance manufacturing site onto a database of pending GMP inspection of a third country active substance manufacturing site.

MHRA will conduct further assessment of the data supplied in the submission(s) at the next routine reinspection of these finished product manufacturing sites.

The entry on the database will be removed if the active substance manufacturing site and the AS subsequently become the subject of a written confirmation, the third country has been assessed as having standards equivalent to GMP, or the AS manufacturing site, following inspection has been issued with a certificate of compliance with EU GMP. The pending-inspection database will only be available as long as this is required as a contingency measure.

Importers of active substances are also asked to note that where the sourcing of active substances from some third countries is difficult because it is not covered by a written confirmation, the exporting country has not been assessed as equivalent and the active substance manufacturing site is not the subject of a valid GMP certificate, these circumstances are subject to on-going review coordinated at an EU level. A key element of this review is the gathering of further data from EU-based finished product manufacturers for active substance import risk assessment and, where required, the EU level coordination of third country active substance manufacturer inspections.

National Contingency Guidance Submission Template

PART A: Finished Product Manufacturer to which this declaration applies

Name and address of MIA holder	Authorisation number

PART B: Concerned Third Country Active Substance Manufacturing Site

Name and Address of Active Substance Manufacturing Site
Name of Active Substances manufactured at this site

PART C: Basis of declaration in lieu of full compliance with Article 46b(2)

Please tick to confirm that an on-site audit of the active substance manufacturer has been conducted by the MIA holder or by a third party on their behalf

(i)   ☐   On-site audit of the active substance manufacturer(s) conducted by MIA holder or by a third party on their behalf:

An on site audit of the active substance(s) manufactured at the site listed in PART B has been completed either by the MIAH(s) listed below or by a third party auditing body i.e. contract acceptor(s) on behalf of the MIAH i.e. contract giver(s) as listed:

MIAH (or contract giver)	Auditing body (contract acceptor)	Site audited	Date of audit[1]

[1]The date of the last audit should not exceed 3 years.

(ii)   Availability of a current[2] certificate of compliance with GMP issued by a recognised national authority or international organisation e.g. EDQM-CEP, US-FDA, EU-MRA partners, EU-ACCA partners, PIC/S member states and the WHO.

☐   A current certificate for the site named in Section B of compliance with GMP issued by a recognised national authority or international organisation is available.

☐   A current certificate for the site named in Section B of compliance with GMP issued by a recognised national authority or international organisation is not available.

Inspection Authority	Date of inspection

[2]The date of the last inspection should not exceed 3 years.

(iii) **Supplementary supportive information (optional):**

For the active substance manufacturing site listed, results of inspection report(s) or GMP certificate(s) issued by recognised national authorities or international organisations together with other supporting information are attached.

Summary of supporting information provided

PART D: Declaration

I declare that:
QP Responsibility

- I am a QP with specific responsibility for GMP compliance of the active substance manufactured at the sites listed in Part B and am authorised to make this declaration.
- That the audit report(s) and all the other documentation relating to this declaration of GMP compliance of the active substance manufacturer(s) will be made available for inspection by the competent authorities, if requested.

GMP Compliance

- The manufacture of the named active substance(s) at the site given in Part B is in accordance with the detailed guideline on good manufacturing practice for active substances used as starting materials as required by Article 46(f) of Directive 2001/83/EC as amended.
- This is based upon an on-site audit of the active substance manufacturer.
- That the outcome of the audit confirms that the active substance manufacturer complies with the principles and guidelines of good manufacturing practice.

Audit

- In the case of third party audit(s), I have evaluated each of the named contract acceptor(s) give in Part C and that technical contractual arrangements are in place and that any measures taken by the contract giver(s) are documented e.g. signed undertakings by the auditor(s).
- In all cases, the audit(s) was/were conducted by properly qualified and trained staff, in accordance with approved procedures.

Inspection, of the third country AS manufacturing site by a recognised national authority or international organisation

- Where available results of inspection report(s) or GMP certificate(s) issued by recognised national authorities or international organisations are within their period of validity and are attached together with other supporting information.

Part E: Name and Signature of QP responsible for this Declaration

This declaration is submitted by:

	Status (job title)
Signatory _____	_____
	MIAH name:
Print name _____	_____
	MIAH number:
Date _____	_____

Legislation on Manufacture and Importation

3

EU Legislation on Manufacture and Importation

Contents

DIRECTIVE 2001/83/EC, TITLE IV, MANUFACTURE AND IMPORTATION

Directive 2001/83/EC of the European Parliament and of the Council of 6 November 2001 on the Community code relating to medicinal products for human use

Title IV: Manufacture and Importation

Editor's note   Title IV of this directive is reproduced below. Reference should be made to the full Directive for the preamble, definitions and the general and final provisions.

Article 46a

1   For the purposes of this Directive, manufacture of active substances used as starting materials shall include both total and partial manufacture or import of an active substance used as a starting material as defined in Part I, point 3.2.1.1 (b) Annex I, and the various processes of dividing up, packaging or presentation prior to its incorporation into a medicinal product, including repackaging or relabelling, such as are carried out by a distributor of starting materials.

2   The Commission shall be empowered to adapt paragraph 1 to take account of scientific and technical progress. That measure, designed to amend non-essential elements of this Directive, shall be adopted in accordance with the regulatory procedure with scrutiny referred to in Article 121(2a).

Article 46b

1   Member States shall take appropriate measures to ensure that the manufacture, import and distribution on their territory of active substances, including active substances that are intended for export, comply with good manufacturing practice and good distribution practices for active substances.

2   Active substances shall only be imported if the following conditions are fulfilled:

(a) the active substances have been manufactured in accordance with standards of good manufacturing practice at least equivalent to those laid down by the Union pursuant to the third paragraph of Article 47; and

(b) the active substances are accompanied by a written confirmation from the competent authority of the exporting third country of the following:

   (i) the standards of good manufacturing practice applicable to the plant manufacturing the exported active substance are at least equivalent to those laid down by the Union pursuant to the third paragraph of Article 47;

   (ii) the manufacturing plant concerned is subject to regular, strict and transparent controls and to the effective enforcement of good manufacturing practice, including repeated and unannounced inspections, so as to ensure a protection of public health at least equivalent to that in the Union; and

   (iii) in the event of findings relating to non-compliance, information on such findings is supplied by the exporting third country to the Union without any delay.

This written confirmation shall be without prejudice to the obligations set out in Article 8 and in point (f) of Article 46.

3 The requirement set out in point (b) of paragraph 2 of this Article shall not apply if the exporting country is included in the list referred to in Article 111b.

4 Exceptionally and where necessary to ensure the availability of medicinal products, when a plant manufacturing an active substance for export has been inspected by a Member State and was found to comply with the principles and guidelines of good manufacturing practice laid down pursuant to the third paragraph of Article 47, the requirement set out in point (b) of paragraph 2 of this Article may be waived by any Member State for a period not exceeding the validity of the certificate of Good Manufacturing Practice. Member States that make use of the possibility of such waiver, shall communicate this to the Commission.

Article 47

The principles and guidelines of good manufacturing practices for medicinal products referred to in Article 46(f) shall be adopted in the form of a directive. That measure, designed to amend non-essential elements of this Directive by supplementing it, shall be adopted in accordance with the regulatory procedure with scrutiny referred to in Article 121(2a).

Detailed guidelines in line with those principles will be published by the Commission and revised necessary to take account of technical and scientific progress.

The Commission shall adopt, by means of delegated acts in accordance with Article 121a and subject to the conditions laid down in Articles 121b and 121c, the principles and guidelines of good manufacturing practice for active substances referred to in the first paragraph of point (f) of Article 46 and in Article 46b.

The principles of good distribution practices for active substances referred to in the first paragraph of point (f) of Article 46 shall be adopted by the Commission in the form of guidelines.

The Commission shall adopt guidelines on the formalised risk assessment for ascertaining the appropriate good manufacturing practice for excipients referred to in the second paragraph of point (f) of Article 46.

Article 52a

1   Importers, manufacturers and distributors of active substances who are established in the Union shall register their activity with the competent authority of the Member State in which they are established.

2   The registration form shall include, at least, the following information:

   (i)   name or corporate name and permanent address;
   (ii)   the active substances which are to be imported, manufactured or distributed;
   (iii) particulars regarding the premises and the technical equipment for their activity.

3   The persons referred to in paragraph 1 shall submit the registration form to the competent authority at least 60 days prior to the intended commencement of their activity.

4   The competent authority may, based on a risk assessment, decide to carry out an inspection. If the competent authority notifies the applicant within 60 days of the receipt of the registration form that an inspection will be carried out, the activity shall not begin before the competent authority has notified the applicant that he may commence the activity. If within 60 days of the receipt of the registration form the competent authority has not notified the applicant that an inspection will be carried out, the applicant may commence the activity.

5   The persons referred to in paragraph 1 shall communicate annually to the competent authority an inventory of the changes which have taken place as regards the information provided in the registration form. Any changes that may have an impact on the quality or safety of the active substances

that are manufactured, imported or distributed must be notified immediately.

6 Persons referred to in paragraph 1 who had commenced their activity before 2 January 2013 shall submit the registration form to the competent authority by 2 March 2013.

7 Member States shall enter the information provided in accordance with paragraph 2 of this Article in the Union database referred to in Article 111(6).

8 This Article shall be without prejudice to Article 111.

Article 52b

1 Notwithstanding Article 2(1), and without prejudice to Title VII, Member States shall take the necessary measures in order to prevent medicinal products that are introduced into the Union, but are not intended to be placed on the market of the Union, from entering into circulation if there are sufficient grounds to suspect that those products are falsified.

2 In order to establish what the necessary measures referred to in paragraph 1 of this Article are, the Commission may adopt, by means of delegated acts in accordance with Article 121a, and subject to the conditions laid down in Articles 121b and 121c, measures supplementing paragraph 1 of this Article as regards the criteria to be considered and the verifications to be made when assessing the potential falsified character of medicinal products introduced into the Union but not intended to be placed on the market.

Article 53

The provisions of this Title shall also apply to homeopathic medicinal products.

UK Legislation on the Manufacture, Importation and Distribution of Active Substances

Contents

The Human Medicines Regulations 2012 (SI 2012/1916)

Editor's note   These extracts from the Human Medicines Regulations 2012 [SI 2012/1916] as amended by the Human Medicines (Amendment) Regulations 2013 [SI 2013/1855] are presented for the reader's convenience. Reproduction is with the permission of HMSO and the Queen's Printer for Scotland. For any definitive information reference must be made to the original Regulations. The numbering and content within this section corresponds with the regulations set out in the published Statutory Instrument (SI 2012 No. 1916) as amended.

Citation and commencement

1 (1) These Regulations may be cited as the Human Medicines Regulations 2012.

(2) These Regulations come into force on 14th August 2012.

General interpretation

8   (1)   In these Regulations (unless the context otherwise requires)-

"active substance" means any substance or mixture of substances intended to be used in the manufacture of a medicinal product and that, when used in its production, becomes an active ingredient of that product intended to exert a pharmacological, immunological or metabolic action with a view to restoring, correcting or modifying physiological functions or to make a medical diagnosis;

"assemble", in relation to a medicinal product or an active substance, includes the various processes of dividing up, packaging and presentation of the product or substance, and "assembly" has a corresponding meaning;

"excipient" means any constituent of a medicinal product other than the active substance and the packaging material;

"export" means export, or attempt to export, from the United Kingdom, whether by land, sea or air;

"falsified medicinal product" means any medicinal product with a false representation of:

(a) its identity, including its packaging and labelling, its name or its composition (other than any unintentional quality defect) as regards any of its ingredients including excipients and the strength of those ingredients;

(b) its source, including its manufacturer, its country of manufacturing, its country of origin or its marketing authorisation holder; or

(c) its history, including the records and documents relating to the distribution channels used;

"import" means import, or attempt to import, into the United Kingdom, whether by land, sea or air;

  (8)   References in these Regulations to:

(a) good manufacturing practice for active substances relate to the principles and guidelines for good manufacturing practice adopted by the European Commission under the third paragraph of Article 47[1] of the 2001 Directive;

(b) good distribution practice for active substances relate to the guidelines on good distribution practices for active substances adopted by the European Commission under the fourth paragraph of Article 47 of the 2001 Directive.

UK LEGISLATION ON
ACTIVE SUBSTANCES

---

[1] Paragraphs 3 and 4 of Article 47 were substituted by Directive 2011/62/EU of the European Parliament and of the Council (OJ No L 174, 1.7.2011, p74).

Chapter 1 Manufacture and distribution of medicinal products and active substances

INTERPRETATION

A17. In this Part "manufacture", in relation to an active substance, includes any process carried out in the course of making the substance and the various processes of dividing up, packaging, and presentation of the active substance.

Chapter 4 Importation, manufacture and distribution of active substances

CRITERIA FOR IMPORTATION, MANUFACTURE OR DISTRIBUTION OF ACTIVE SUBSTANCES

45M. (1) A person may not:
(a) import;
(b) manufacture; or
(c) distribute,
an active substance unless that person is registered with the licensing authority in accordance with regulation 45N and the requirements in regulation 45O are met.
(2) Paragraph (1) applies in relation to an active substance which is to be used in an investigational medicinal product only:
(a) if the product has a marketing authorisation, Article 126a authorisation, certificate of registration or traditional herbal registration; and
(b) to the extent that the manufacture of the active substance is in accordance with the terms and conditions of that authorisation, certificate or registration.
(3) Paragraph (1)(a) does not apply to a person who, in connection with the importation of an active substance from a state other than an EEA state:
(a) provides facilities solely for transporting the active substance; or
(b) acting as an import agent, imports the active substance solely to the order of another person who holds a certificate of good manufacturing practice issued by the licensing authority.

Registration in relation to active substances

45N. (1) For registration in relation to active substances, the licensing authority must have received a valid registration form from the applicant for import, manufacture or, as the case may be, distribution of the active substance and:

(a) 60 days have elapsed since receipt and the licensing authority have not notified the applicant that an inspection will be carried out; or

(b) the licensing authority:

    (i) notified the applicant within 60 days of receipt of a registration form that an inspection will be carried out; and

    (ii) within 90 days of that inspection the licensing authority have issued that person with a certificate of good manufacturing practice or, as the case may be, of good distribution practice; and

(c) that person has not instructed the licensing authority to end that person's registration.

(2) The person applying for registration under paragraph (1) must notify the licensing authority of any changes which have taken place as regards the information in the registration form:

(a) immediately where such changes may have an impact on quality or safety of the active substances that are manufactured, imported or distributed;

(b) in any other case, on each anniversary of the receipt of the application form by the licensing authority.

(3) For the purpose of paragraph (2), changes which are notified in accordance with that paragraph shall be treated as incorporated in the application form.

(4) Any notification to the licensing authority under paragraph (2) must be accompanied by the appropriate fee in accordance with the Fees Regulations.

(5) A registration form is valid for the purpose of paragraph (1) if:

(a) it is provided to the licensing authority; and

(b) is completed in the way and form specified in Schedule 7A.

(6) Paragraph (1) does not apply until 20th October 2013 in relation to a person who had, before 20th August 2013, commenced the activity for which the person would, apart from this provision, need to send a registration form to the licensing authority.

Requirements for registration as an importer, manufacturer or distributor of an active substance

45O. (1) Where the Commission has adopted principles and guidelines of good manufacturing practice under the third paragraph of Article 47[2] of the 2001 Directive which applies to an active substance manufactured in the UK, the manufacturer must comply with good manufacturing practice in relation to that active substance.

---

[2] Article 47 was amended by Directive 2011/62/EU of the European Parliament and of the Council (OJ No L 174, 1.7.2011, p74).

(2) Where the Commission has adopted principles and guidelines of good distribution practice under the fourth paragraph of Article 47 of the 2001 Directive which applies to an active substance distributed in the United Kingdom, the distributor must comply with good distribution practice in relation to that active substance.

(3) Without prejudice to regulation 37(4) (manufacture and assembly in relation to active substances) and paragraph 9A of Schedule 8 (material to accompany an application for a UK marketing authorisation in relation to an active substance), where the Commission has adopted principles and guidelines of good manufacturing practice under the third paragraph of Article 47 of the 2001 Directive which applies to an active substance imported into the UK and where an active substance is imported from a third country:

   (a) the importer must comply with good manufacturing practice and good distribution practice in relation to the active substance;

   (b) the active substances must have been manufactured in accordance with standards which are at least equivalent to good manufacturing practice; and

   (c) the active substances must be accompanied by a written confirmation from the competent authority of the exporting third country of the following:

      (i) the standards of manufacturing practice applicable to the plant manufacturing the exported active substance are at least equivalent to good manufacturing practice,

      (ii) the manufacturing plant concerned is subject to regular, strict and transparent controls and to the effective enforcement of standards of manufacturing practice at least equivalent to good manufacturing practice, including repeated and unannounced inspections, so as to ensure a protection of public health at least equivalent to that in the Union, and

      (iii) in the event of findings relating to non-compliance, information on such findings is supplied by the exporting third country to the Union without any delay.

(4) Paragraph (3)(c) does not apply:

   (a) where the country from where the active substance is exported is included in the list referred to in Article 111b of the 2001 Directive; or

   (b) for a period not exceeding the validity of the certificate of good manufacturing practice, where:

      (i) in relation to a plant where active substances are manufactured where the competent authority of a member State has found, upon inspection, that a plant complies with the principles and guidelines of good manufacturing practice, and

   (ii) the licensing authority is of the opinion that it is necessary to waive the requirement to ensure availability of the active substance.

(5) The criteria in this regulation apply regardless of whether an active substance is intended for export.

Provision of information

45P. (1) In this regulation:

"R" means a person who is, or has applied to the licensing authority to become, a registered importer, manufacturer or distributor of active substances;

"reporting year" means a period of twelve months ending on 31st March.

(2) On or before the date specified in paragraph (3), R must submit a report to the licensing authority which:

 (a) includes a declaration that R has in place an appropriate system to ensure compliance with regulations 45N, 45O and this regulation; and

 (b) details the system which R has in place to ensure such compliance.

(3) The date specified for the purposes of this paragraph is:

 (a) in relation to any application made before 31st March 2014, the date of the application; and

 (b) in relation to each subsequent reporting year, 30th April following the end of that year.

(4) R must without delay notify the licensing authority of any changes to the matters in respect of which evidence has been supplied in relation to paragraph (2) which might affect compliance with the requirements of this Chapter.

(5) Any report or notification to the licensing authority under paragraph (2) or (4) must be accompanied by the appropriate fee in accordance with the Fees Regulations.

(6) The licensing authority may give a notice to R, requiring R to provide information of a kind specified in the notice within the period specified in the notice.

(7) A notice under paragraph (6) may not be given to R unless it appears to the licensing authority that it is necessary for the licensing authority to consider whether the registration should be varied, suspended or removed from the active substance register.

(8) A notice under paragraph (6) may specify information which the licensing authority thinks necessary for considering whether the registration should be varied, suspended or removed from the active substance register.

Schedule 7A - Information to be provided for registration as an importer, manufacturer or distributor of active substances

(1) The name and address of the applicant.

(2) The name and address of the person (if any) making the application on the applicant's behalf.

(3) The address of each of the premises where any operations to which the registration relates are to be carried out.

(4) The address of any premises not mentioned by virtue of the above requirement, where:

    (a) the applicant proposes to keep any living animals, from which substance(s) used in the production of the active substance(s) to which the application relates are to be derived;

    (b) materials of animal origin from which an active substance is to be derived, as mentioned in the above sub-paragraph, are to be kept.

(5) The address of each of the premises where active substances are to be stored, or from which active substances are to be distributed.

(6) The address of each of the premises where any testing associated with the manufacture or assembly of active substances to which the registration relates.

(7) The name, address, qualifications and experience of the person whose duty it will be to supervise any manufacturing operations, and the name and job title of the person to whom they report.

(8) The name, address, qualifications and experience of the person who will have responsibility for the quality control of active substances, and the name and job title of the person to whom they report.

(9) The name, address, qualifications and experience of the person whose duty it will be to supervise any importation, storage or distribution operations, and the name and job title of the person to whom they report.

(10) The name, address and qualifications of the person to be responsible for any animals kept as mentioned in paragraph 4(a).

(11) The name, address and qualifications of the person to be responsible for the culture of any living tissue for use in the manufacture of an active substance.

(12) For each active substance to be manufactured, imported, or distributed:

    (a) the CAS registration number[3] assigned to that active substance by the Chemical Abstracts Service, a division of the American Chemical Society;

---

[3] Further information is available from the website of the Chemical Abstracts Service at www.cas.org.

(b) where applicable, the Anatomical Therapeutic Category code[4] assigned to that active substance under the Anatomical Therapeutic Chemical Classification System used for the classification of drugs by the World Health Organisation's Collaborating Centre for Drug Statistics Methodology;

(c) either:

(i) the International Union of Pure and Applied Chemistry nomenclature, or

(ii) the common name; and

(d) the intended quantities of each active substance to be manufactured, imported or distributed.

(13) Details of the operations to which the registration relates, including a statement of whether they include:

(a) the manufacture of active substances;

(b) the importation of active substances from third countries;

(c) the storage of active substances; or

(d) the distribution of active substances.

(14) A statement of the facilities and equipment available at each of the premises where active substances are to be manufactured, stored or distributed.

(15) A statement as to whether the particular active substances are intended for:

(a) use in a medicinal product with an EU marketing authorisation;

(b) use in a special medicinal product; or

(c) export to a third country.

(16) A separate statement in respect of each of the premises mentioned in the application of:

(a) the manufacturing, storage or distribution operations carried out at those sites, and the specific active substances to which those activities relate; and

(b) the equipment available at those premises for carrying out those activities.

(17) A statement of the authority conferred on the person responsible for quality control to reject unsatisfactory active substances.

(18) A description of the arrangements for the identification and storage of materials before and during the manufacture of active substances.

(19) A description of the arrangements for the identification and storage of active substances.

(20) A description of the arrangements at each of the premises where the applicant proposes to store active substances for ensuring, as far as practicable, the turn-over of stocks of active substances.

---

[4] Further information is available from the website of the WHO Collaborating Centre for Drug Statistics Methodology at www.whocc.no.

(21) A description of the arrangements for maintaining:
   (a) production records, including records of manufacture and assembly;
   (b) records of analytical and other tests used in the course of manufacture or assembly for ensuring compliance of materials used in manufacture, or of active substances, with the specification for such materials or active substances;
   (c) records of importation;
   (d) records of storage and distribution.
(22) A description of the arrangements for keeping reference samples of:
   (a) materials used in the manufacture of active substances; and
   (b) active substances.
(23) Where the application relates to active substances intended for use in an advanced therapy medicinal product, an outline of the arrangements for maintaining records to allow traceability containing sufficient detail to enable the linking of an active substance to the advanced therapy medicinal product it was used in the manufacture of and vice versa.
(24) Details of:
   (a) any manufacturing, importation, storage or distribution operations, other than those to which the application for registration relates, carried on by the applicant on or near each of the premises, and
   (b) the substances or articles to which those operations relate.

Guidance on Wholesale Distribution Practice and Brokering Medicines

Guidelines on Good Distribution Practice of Medicinal Products for Human Use (2013/C 343/01)

Contents

Guidelines on Good Distribution Practice of Medicinal Products for Human Use (2013/C 343/01)

These Guidelines are based on Article 84 and Article 85b(3) of Directive 2001/83/EC[1].

The Commission has published EU Guidelines on Good Distribution Practice (GDP) in 1994[2]. Revised guidelines were published in March 2013[3] in order to take into account recent advances in practices for appropriate storage and distribution of medicinal products in the European Union, as well as new requirements introduced by Directive 2011/62/EU[4].

This version corrects factual mistakes identified in subchapters 5.5 and 6.3 of the revised guidelines. It also gives more explanations on the rationale for the revision as well as a date of coming into operation.

It replaces the guidelines on GDP published in March 2013.

The wholesale distribution of medicinal products is an important activity in integrated supply chain management. Today's distribution network for medicinal products is increasingly complex and involves many players. These Guidelines lay down appropriate tools to assist wholesale distributors in conducting their activities and to prevent falsified medicines from entering the legal supply chain. Compliance with these Guidelines will ensure control of the distribution chain and consequently maintain the quality and the integrity of medicinal products.

According to Article 1(17) of Directive 2001/83/EC, wholesale distribution of medicinal products is 'all activities consisting of procuring, holding, supplying or exporting medicinal products, apart from supplying medicinal products to the public. Such activities are carried out with manufacturers or their depositories, importers, other wholesale distributors or with pharmacists and persons authorized or entitled to supply medicinal products to the public in the Member State concerned'.

Any person acting as a wholesale distributor has to hold a wholesale distribution authorisation. Article 80(g) of Directive 2001/83/EC provides that distributors must comply with the principle of and guidelines for GDP.

---

[1] Directive 2001/83/EC of the European Parliament and of the Council of 6 November 2001 on the Community code relating to medicinal products for human use, OJ L 311, 28.11.2001, p. 67.

[2] Guidelines on Good Distribution Practice of medicinal products for human use, OJ C 63, 1.3.1994, p. 4.

[3] Guidelines of 7 March 2013 on Good Distribution Practice of medicinal products for human use, OJ C 68, 8.3.2013, p. 1.

[4] Directive 2011/62/EU of the European Parliament and of the Council amending Directive 2001/83/EC as regards the prevention of the entry into the legal supply chain of falsified medicinal products, OJ L 174, 1.7.2011, p. 74.

Possession of a manufacturing authorisation includes authorisation to distribute the medicinal products covered by the authorisation. Manufacturers performing any distribution activities with their own products must therefore comply with GDP.

The definition of wholesale distribution does not depend on whether that distributor is established or operating in specific customs areas, such as in free zones or in free warehouses. All obligations related to wholesale distribution activities (such as exporting, holding or supplying) also apply to these distributors. Relevant sections of these Guidelines should also be adhered to by other actors involved in the distribution of medicinal products.

Other actors such as brokers may also play a role in the distribution channel for medicinal products. According to Article 85(b) of Directive 2001/83/EC, persons brokering medicinal products must be subject to certain provisions applicable to wholesale distributors, as well as specific provisions on brokering.

Chapter 1 – Quality Management

1.1 Principle

Wholesale distributors must maintain a quality system setting out responsibilities, processes and risk management principles in relation to their activities[1]. All distribution activities should be clearly defined and systematically reviewed. All critical steps of distribution processes and significant changes should be justified and where relevant validated. The quality system is the responsibility of the organisation's management and requires their leadership and active participation and should be supported by staff commitment.

1.2 Quality system

The system for managing quality should encompass the organisational structure, procedures, processes and resources, as well as activities necessary to ensure confidence that the product delivered maintains its quality and integrity and remains within the legal supply chain during storage and/or transportation.

The quality system should be fully documented and its effectiveness monitored. All quality system-related activities should be defined and documented. A quality manual or equivalent documentation approach should be established.

---

[1] Article 80(h) of Directive 2001/83/EC.

A responsible person should be appointed by the management, who should have clearly specified authority and responsibility for ensuring that a quality system is implemented and maintained.

The management of the distributor should ensure that all parts of the quality system are adequately resourced with competent personnel, and suitable and sufficient premises, equipment and facilities.

The size, structure and complexity of distributor's activities should be taken into consideration when developing or modifying the quality system.

A change control system should be in place. This system should incorporate quality risk management principles, and be proportionate and effective.

The quality system should ensure that:

(i)   medicinal products are procured, held, supplied or exported in a way that is compliant with the requirements of GDP;
(ii)   management responsibilities are clearly specified;
(iii) products are delivered to the right recipients within a satisfactory time period;
(iv)   records are made contemporaneously;
(v)   deviations from established procedures are documented and investigated;
(vi)   appropriate corrective and preventive actions (commonly known as 'CAPA') are taken to correct deviations and prevent them in line with the principles of quality risk management.

1.3   Management of outsourced activities

The quality system should extend to the control and review of any outsourced activities related to the procurement, holding, supply or export of medicinal products. These processes should incorporate quality risk management and include:

(i)   assessing the suitability and competence of the contract acceptor to carry out the activity and checking authorisation status, if required;
(ii)   defining the responsibilities and communication processes for the quality-related activities of the parties involved;
(iii) monitoring and review of the performance of the contract acceptor, and the identification and implementation of any required improvements on a regular basis.

1.4   Management review and monitoring

The management should have a formal process for reviewing the quality system on a periodic basis. The review should include:

(i)   measurement of the achievement of quality system objectives;
(ii) assessment of performance indicators that can be used to monitor the effectiveness of processes within the quality system, such as complaints, deviations, CAPA, changes to processes; feedback on outsourced activities; self-assessment processes including risk assessments and audits; and external assessments such as inspections, findings and customer audits;
(iii) emerging regulations, guidance and quality issues that can impact the quality management system;
(iv) innovations that might enhance the quality system;
(v)   changes in business environment and objectives.

The outcome of each management review of the quality system should be documented in a timely manner and effectively communicated internally.

1.5   Quality risk management

Quality risk management is a systematic process for the assessment, control, communication and review of risks to the quality of medicinal products. It can be applied both proactively and retrospectively.

Quality risk management should ensure that the evaluation of the risk to quality is based on scientific knowledge, experience with the process and ultimately links to the protection of the patient. The level of effort, formality and documentation of the process should be commensurate with the level of risk. Examples of the processes and applications of quality risk management can be found in guideline Q9 of the International Conference on Harmonisation ('ICH').

Chapter 2 – Personnel

2.1   Principle

The correct distribution of medicinal products relies upon people. For this reason, there must be sufficient competent personnel to carry out all the tasks for which the wholesale distributor is responsible. Individual responsibilities should be clearly understood by the staff and be recorded.

2.2   Responsible person

The wholesale distributor must designate a person as responsible person. The responsible person should meet the qualifications and all conditions provided for by the legislation of the Member State concerned[1]. A degree in

---

[1] Article 79(b) of Directive 2001/83/EC.

EU GDP CHAPTER 2 PERSONNEL

pharmacy is desirable. The responsible person should have appropriate competence and experience as well as knowledge of and training in GDP.

The responsible person should fulfil their responsibilities personally and should be continuously contactable. The responsible person may delegate duties but not responsibilities.

The written job description of the responsible person should define their authority to take decisions with regard to their responsibilities. The wholesale distributor should give the responsible person the defined authority, resources and responsibility needed to fulfil their duties.

The responsible person should carry out their duties in such a way as to ensure that the wholesale distributor can demonstrate GDP compliance and that public service obligations are met.

The responsibilities of the responsible person include:

(i)   ensuring that a quality management system is implemented and maintained;

(ii)   focusing on the management of authorised activities and the accuracy and quality of records;

(iii)   ensuring that initial and continuous training programmes are implemented and maintained;

(iv)   coordinating and promptly performing any recall operations for medicinal products;

(v)   ensuring that relevant customer complaints are dealt with effectively;

(vi)   ensuring that suppliers and customers are approved;

(vii)   approving any subcontracted activities which may impact on GDP;

(viii) ensuring that self-inspections are performed at appropriate regular intervals following a prearranged programme and necessary corrective measures are put in place;

(ix)   keeping appropriate records of any delegated duties;

(x)   deciding on the final disposition of returned, rejected, recalled or falsified products;

(xi)   approving any returns to saleable stock;

(xii)   ensuring that any additional requirements imposed on certain products by national law are adhered to[2].

2.3 Other personnel

There should be an adequate number of competent personnel involved in all stages of the wholesale distribution activities of medicinal products. The number of personnel required will depend on the volume and scope of activities.

---

[2] Article 83 of Directive 2001/83/EC.

The organisational structure of the wholesale distributor should be set out in an organisation chart. The role, responsibilities, and interrelationships of all personnel should be clearly indicated.

The role and responsibilities of employees working in key positions should be set out in written job descriptions, along with any arrangements for deputising.

2.4 Training

All personnel involved in wholesale distribution activities should be trained on the requirements of GDP. They should have the appropriate competence and experience prior to commencing their tasks.

Personnel should receive initial and continuing training relevant to their role, based on written procedures and in accordance with a written training programme. The responsible person should also maintain their competence in GDP through regular training.

In addition, training should include aspects of product identification and avoidance of falsified medicines entering the supply chain.

Personnel dealing with any products which require more stringent handling conditions should receive specific training. Examples of such products include hazardous products, radioactive materials, products presenting special risks of abuse (including narcotic and psychotropic substances), and temperature-sensitive products.

A record of all training should be kept, and the effectiveness of training should be periodically assessed and documented.

2.5 Hygiene

Appropriate procedures relating to personnel hygiene, relevant to the activities being carried out, should be established and observed. Such procedures should cover health, hygiene and clothing.

Chapter 3 – Premises and Equipment

3.1 Principle

Wholesale distributors must have suitable and adequate premises, installations and equipment[1], so as to ensure proper storage and distribution of medicinal products. In particular, the premises should be clean, dry and maintained within acceptable temperature limits.

---

[1] Article 79(a) of Directive 2001/83/EC.

EU GDP CHAPTER 3 PREMISES AND EQUIPMENT

3.2 Premises

The premises should be designed or adapted to ensure that the required storage conditions are maintained. They should be suitably secure, structurally sound and of sufficient capacity to allow safe storage and handling of the medicinal products. Storage areas should be provided with adequate lighting to enable all operations to be carried out accurately and safely.

Where premises are not directly operated by the wholesale distributor, a contract should be in place. The contracted premises should be covered by a separate wholesale distribution authorisation.

Medicinal products should be stored in segregated areas which are clearly marked and have access restricted to authorised personnel. Any system replacing physical segregation, such as electronic segregation based on a computerised system, should provide equivalent security and should be validated.

Products pending a decision as to their disposition or products that have been removed from saleable stock should be segregated either physically or through an equivalent electronic system. This includes, for example, any product suspected of falsification and returned products. Medicinal products received from a third country but not intended for the Union market should also be physically segregated. Any falsified medicinal products, expired products, recalled products and rejected products found in the supply chain should be immediately physically segregated and stored in a dedicated area away from all other medicinal products. The appropriate degree of security should be applied in these areas to ensure that such items remain separate from saleable stock. These areas should be clearly identified.

Special attention should be paid to the storage of products with specific handling instructions as specified in national law. Special storage conditions (and special authorisations) may be required for such products (e.g. narcotics and psychotropic substances).

Radioactive materials and other hazardous products, as well as products presenting special safety risks of fire or explosion (e.g. medicinal gases, combustibles, flammable liquids and solids), should be stored in one or more dedicated areas subject to local legislation and appropriate safety and security measures.

Receiving and dispatch bays should protect products from prevailing weather conditions. There should be adequate separation between the receipt and dispatch and storage areas. Procedures should be in place to maintain control of inbound/outbound goods. Reception areas where deliveries are examined following receipt should be designated and suitably equipped.

Unauthorised access to all areas of the authorised premises should be prevented. Prevention measures would usually include a monitored intruder alarm system and appropriate access control. Visitors should be accompanied.

Premises and storage facilities should be clean and free from litter and dust. Cleaning programmes, instructions and records should be in place. Appropriate cleaning equipment and cleaning agents should be chosen and used so as not to present a source of contamination.

Premises should be designed and equipped so as to afford protection against the entry of insects, rodents or other animals. A preventive pest control programme should be in place.

Rest, wash and refreshment rooms for employees should be adequately separated from the storage areas. The presence of food, drink, smoking material or medicinal products for personal use should be prohibited in the storage areas.

3.2.1. TEMPERATURE AND ENVIRONMENT CONTROL

Suitable equipment and procedures should be in place to check the environment where medicinal products are stored. Environmental factors to be considered include temperature, light, humidity and cleanliness of the premises.

An initial temperature mapping exercise should be carried out on the storage area before use, under representative conditions. Temperature monitoring equipment should be located according to the results of the mapping exercise, ensuring that monitoring devices are positioned in the areas that experience the extremes of fluctuations. The mapping exercise should be repeated according to the results of a risk assessment exercise or whenever significant modifications are made to the facility or the temperature controlling equipment. For small premises of a few square meters which are at room temperature, an assessment of potential risks (e.g. heaters) should be conducted and temperature monitors placed accordingly.

3.3 Equipment

All equipment impacting on storage and distribution of medicinal products should be designed, located and maintained to a standard which suits its intended purpose. Planned maintenance should be in place for key equipment vital to the functionality of the operation.

Equipment used to control or to monitor the environment where the medicinal products are stored should be calibrated at defined intervals based on a risk and reliability assessment.

Calibration of equipment should be traceable to a national or international measurement standard. Appropriate alarm systems should be in place to provide alerts when there are excursions from pre-defined storage conditions. Alarm levels should be appropriately set and alarms should be regularly tested to ensure adequate functionality.

Equipment repair, maintenance and calibration operations should be carried out in such a way that the integrity of the medicinal products is not compromised.

Adequate records of repair, maintenance and calibration activities for key equipment should be made and the results should be retained. Key equipment would include for example cold stores, monitored intruder alarm and access control systems, refrigerators, thermo hygrometers, or other temperature and humidity recording devices, air handling units and any equipment used in conjunction with the onward supply chain.

3.3.1. COMPUTERISED SYSTEMS

Before a computerised system is brought into use, it should be demonstrated, through appropriate validation or verification studies, that the system is capable of achieving the desired results accurately, consistently and reproducibly.

A written, detailed description of the system should be available (including diagrams where appropriate). This should be kept up to date. The document should describe principles, objectives, security measures, system scope and main features, how the computerised system is used and the way it interacts with other systems.

Data should only be entered into the computerised system or amended by persons authorised to do so.

Data should be secured by physical or electronic means and protected against accidental or unauthorised modifications. Stored data should be checked periodically for accessibility. Data should be protected by backing up at regular intervals. Back up data should be retained for the period stated in national legislation but at least five years at a separate and secure location.

Procedures to be followed if the system fails or breaks down should be defined. This should include systems for the restoration of data.

3.3.2. QUALIFICATION AND VALIDATION

Wholesale distributors should identify what key equipment qualification and/or key process validation is necessary to ensure correct installation and operation. The scope and extent of such qualification and/or validation activities (such as storage, pick and pack processes) should be determined using a documented risk assessment approach.

Equipment and processes should be respectively qualified and/or validated before commencing use and after any significant changes e.g. repair or maintenance.

Validation and qualification reports should be prepared summarising the results obtained and commenting on any observed deviations. Deviations from established procedures should be documented and further actions decided to correct deviations and avoid their reoccurrence (corrective and preventive actions). The principles of CAPA should be applied where necessary. Evidence of satisfactory validation and acceptance of a process or piece of equipment should be produced and approved by appropriate personnel.

Chapter 4 – Documentation

4.1 Principle

Good documentation constitutes an essential part of the quality system. Written documentation should prevent errors from spoken communication and permits the tracking of relevant operations during the distribution of medicinal products.

4.2 General

Documentation comprises all written procedures, instructions, contracts, records and data, in paper or in electronic form. Documentation should be readily available/retrievable.

With regard to the processing of personal data of employees, complainants or any other natural person, Directive 95/46/EC[1] on the protection of individuals applies to the processing of personal data and to the free movement of such data.

Documentation should be sufficiently comprehensive with respect to the scope of the wholesale distributor's activities and in a language understood by personnel. It should be written in clear, unambiguous language and be free from errors.

Procedure should be approved signed and dated by the responsible person. Documentation should be approved, signed and dated by appropriate authorised persons, as required. It should not be hand-written; although, where it is necessary, sufficient space should be provided for such entries.

[1] OJ L 281, 23.11.1995, p. 31.

EU GDP CHAPTER 4
DOCUMENTATION

Any alteration made in the documentation should be signed and dated; the alteration should permit the reading of the original information. Where appropriate, the reason for the alteration should be recorded.

Documents should be retained for the period stated in national legislation but at least five years. Personal data should be deleted or anonymised as soon as their storage is no longer than necessary for the purpose of distribution activities.

Each employee should have ready access to all necessary documentation for the tasks executed.

Attention should be paid to using valid and approved procedures. Documents should have unambiguous content; title, nature and purpose should be clearly stated. Documents should be reviewed regularly and kept up to date. Version control should be applied to procedures. After revision of a document a system should exist to prevent inadvertent use of the superseded version. Superseded or obsolete procedures should be removed from workstations and archived.

Records must be kept either in the form of purchase/sales invoices, delivery slips, or on computer or any other form, for any transaction in medicinal products received, supplied or brokered.

Records must include at least the following information: date; name of the medicinal product; quantity received, supplied or brokered; name and address of the supplier, customer, broker or consignee, as appropriate; and batch number at least for medicinal product bearing the safety features[2].

Records should be made at the time each operation is undertaken.

Chapter 5 – Operations

5.1 Principle

All actions taken by wholesale distributors should ensure that the identity of the medicinal product is not lost and that the wholesale distribution of medicinal products is performed according to the information on the outer packaging. The wholesale distributor should use all means available to minimise the risk of falsified medicinal products entering the legal supply chain.

All medicinal products distributed in the EU by a wholesale distributor must be covered by a marketing authorisation granted by the EU or by a Member State[3].

Any distributor, other than the marketing authorisation holder, who imports a medicinal product from another Member State must notify the marketing authorisation holder and the competent authority in the

---

[2] Articles 80(e) and 82 of Directive 2001/83/EC.
[3] Articles 76(1) and (2) of Directive 2001/83/EC.

Member State to which the medicinal product will be imported of their intention to import that product[4]. All key operations described below should be fully described in the quality system in appropriate documentation.

5.2 Qualification of suppliers

Wholesale distributors must obtain their supplies of medicinal products only from persons who are themselves in possession of a wholesale distribution authorisation, or who are in possession of a manufacturing authorisation which covers the product in question[5].

Wholesale distributors receiving medicinal products from third countries for the purpose of importation, i.e. for the purpose of placing these products on the EU market, must hold a manufacturing authorisation[6].

Where medicinal products are obtained from another wholesale distributor the receiving wholesale distributor must verify that the supplier complies with the principles and guidelines of good distribution practices and that they hold an authorisation for example by using the Union database. If the medicinal product is obtained through brokering, the wholesale distributor must verify that the broker is registered and complies with the requirements in Chapter 10[1].

Appropriate qualification and approval of suppliers should be performed prior to any procurement of medicinal products. This should be controlled by a procedure and the results documented and periodically rechecked.

When entering into a new contract with new suppliers the wholesale distributor should carry out 'due diligence' checks in order to assess the suitability, competence and reliability of the other party. Attention should be paid to:

(i)   the reputation or reliability of the supplier;
(ii)   offers of medicinal products more likely to be falsified;
(iii)   large offers of medicinal products which are generally only available in limited quantities; and
(iv)   out-of-range prices.

---

[4] Article 76(3) of Directive 2001/83/EC.
[5] Article 80(b) of Directive 2001/83/EC.
[6] Article 40, third paragraph of Directive 2001/83/EC.
[1] Article 80, fourth paragraph of Directive 2001/83/EC.

5.3   Qualification of customers

Wholesale distributors must ensure they supply medicinal products only to persons who are themselves in possession of a wholesale distribution authorisation or who are authorised or entitled to supply medicinal products to the public.

Checks and periodic rechecks may include: requesting copies of customer's authorisations according to national law, verifying status on an authority website, requesting evidence of qualifications or entitlement according to national legislation.

Wholesale distributors should monitor their transactions and investigate any irregularity in the sales patterns of narcotics, psychotropic substances or other dangerous substances. Unusual sales patterns that may constitute diversion or misuse of medicinal product should be investigated and reported to competent authorities where necessary. Steps should be taken to ensure fulfilment of any public service obligation imposed upon them.

5.4   Receipt of medicinal products

The purpose of the receiving function is to ensure that the arriving consignment is correct, that the medicinal products originate from approved suppliers and that they have not been visibly damaged during transport.

Medicinal products requiring special storage or security measures should be prioritised and once appropriate checks have been conducted they should be immediately transferred to appropriate storage facilities.

Batches of medicinal products intended for the EU and EEA countries should not be transferred to saleable stock before assurance has been obtained in accordance with written procedures, that they are authorised for sale. For batches coming from another Member State, prior to their transfer to saleable stock, the control report referred to in Article 51(1) of Directive 2001/83/EC or another proof of release to the market in question based on an equivalent system should be carefully checked by appropriately trained personnel.

5.5   Storage

Medicinal products and, if necessary, healthcare products should be stored separately from other products likely to alter them and should be protected from the harmful effects of light, temperature, moisture and other external factors. Particular attention should be paid to products requiring specific storage conditions.

Incoming containers of medicinal products should be cleaned, if necessary, before storage.

Warehousing operations must ensure appropriate storage conditions are maintained and allow for appropriate security of stocks.

Stock should be rotated according to the 'first expiry, first out' (FEFO) principle. Exceptions should be documented.

Medicinal products should be handled and stored in such a manner as to prevent spillage, breakage, contamination and mix-ups. Medicinal products should not be stored directly on the floor unless the package is designed to allow such storage (such as for some medicinal gas cylinders).

Medicinal products that are nearing their expiry date/shelf life should be withdrawn immediately from saleable stock either physically or through other equivalent electronic segregation.

Stock inventories should be performed regularly taking into account national legislation requirements. Stock irregularities should be investigated and documented.

5.6 Destruction of obsolete goods

Medicinal products intended for destruction should be appropriately identified, held separately and handled in accordance with a written procedure.

Destruction of medicinal products should be in accordance with national or international requirements for handling, transport and disposal of such products.

Records of all destroyed medicinal products should be retained for a defined period.

5.7 Picking

Controls should be in place to ensure the correct product is picked. The product should have an appropriate remaining shelf life when it is picked.

5.8 Supply

For all supplies, a document (e.g. delivery note) must be enclosed stating the date; name and pharmaceutical form of the medicinal product, batch number at least for products bearing the safety features; quantity supplied; name and address of the supplier, name and delivery address of the consignee[1] (actual physical storage premises, if different) and applicable transport and storage conditions. Records should be kept so that the actual location of the product can be known.

---

[1] Article 82 of Directive 2001/83/EC.

5.9   Export to third countries

The export of medicinal products falls within the definition of 'wholesale distribution'[2]. A person exporting medicinal products must hold a wholesale distribution authorisation or a manufacturing authorisation. This is also the case if the exporting wholesale distributor is operating from a free zone.

The rules for wholesale distribution apply in their entirety in the case of export of medicinal products. However, where medicinal products are exported, they do not need to be covered by a marketing authorisation of the Union or a Member State[3]. Wholesalers should take the appropriate measures in order to prevent these medicinal products reaching the Union market. Where wholesale distributors supply medicinal products to persons in third countries, they shall ensure that such supplies are only made to persons who are authorised or entitled to receive medicinal products for wholesale distribution or supply to the public in accordance with the applicable legal and administrative provisions of the country concerned.

Chapter 6 – Complaints, Returns, Suspected Falsified Medicinal Products and Medicinal Product Recalls

6.1   Principle

All complaints, returns, suspected falsified medicinal products and recalls must be recorded and handled carefully according to written procedures. Records should be made available to the competent authorities. An assessment of returned medicinal products should be performed before any approval for resale. A consistent approach by all partners in the supply chain is required in order to be successful in the fight against falsified medicinal products.

6.2   Complaints

Complaints should be recorded with all the original details. A distinction should be made between complaints related to the quality of a medicinal product and those related to distribution. In the event of a complaint about the quality of a medicinal product and a potential product defect, the manufacturer and/or marketing authorisation holder should be informed without delay. Any product distribution complaint should be thoroughly investigated to identify the origin of or reason for the complaint.

---

[2] Article 1(17) of Directive 2001/83/EC.
[3] Article 85(a) of Directive 2001/83/EC.

A person should be appointed to handle complaints and allocated sufficient support personnel.

If necessary, appropriate follow-up actions (including CAPA) should be taken after investigation and evaluation of the complaint, including where required notification to the national competent authorities.

6.3   Returned medicinal products

Returned products must be handled according to a written, risk-based process taking into account the product concerned, any specific storage requirements and the time elapsed since the medicinal product was originally dispatched. Returns should be conducted in accordance with national law and contractual arrangements between the parties.

Medicinal products which have left the premises of the distributor should only be returned to saleable stock if all of the following are confirmed:

(i)   the medicinal products are in their unopened and undamaged secondary packaging and are in good condition; have not expired and have not been recalled;

(ii)   medicinal products returned from a customer not holding a wholesale distribution authorisation or from pharmacies authorised to supply medicinal products to the public should only be returned to saleable stock if they are returned within an acceptable time limit, for example 10 days.

(iii)   it has been demonstrated by the customer that the medicinal products have been transported, stored and handled in compliance with their specific storage requirements;

(iv)   they have been examined and assessed by a sufficiently trained and competent person authorised to do so;

(v)   the distributor has reasonable evidence that the product was supplied to that customer (via copies of the original delivery note or by referencing invoice numbers, etc.) and the batch number for products bearing the safety features is known, and that there is no reason to believe that the product has been falsified.

Moreover, for medicinal products requiring specific temperature storage conditions such as low temperature, returns to saleable stock can only be made if there is documented evidence that the product has been stored under the authorised storage conditions throughout the entire time. If any deviation has occurred a risk assessment has to be performed, on which basis the integrity of the product can be demonstrated. The evidence should cover:

(i)   delivery to customer;

(ii)   examination of the product;
(iii) opening of the transport packaging;
(iv)   return of the product to the packaging;
(v)   collection and return to the distributor;
(vi)   return to the distribution site refrigerator.

Products returned to saleable stock should be placed such that the 'first expired first out' (FEFO) system operates effectively.

Stolen products that have been recovered cannot be returned to saleable stock and sold to customers.

6.4   Falsified medicinal products

Wholesale distributors must immediately inform the competent authority and the marketing authorisation holder of any medicinal products they identify as falsified or suspect to be falsified[1]. A procedure should be in place to this effect. It should be recorded with all the original details and investigated.

Any falsified medicinal products found in the supply chain should immediately be physically segregated and stored in a dedicated area away from all other medicinal products. All relevant activities in relation to such products should be documented and records retained.

6.5   Medicinal product recalls

The effectiveness of the arrangements for product recall should be evaluated regularly (at least annually).

Recall operations should be capable of being initiated promptly and at any time.

The distributor must follow the instructions of a recall message, which should be approved, if required, by the competent authorities.

Any recall operation should be recorded at the time it is carried out. Records should be made readily available to the competent authorities.

The distribution records should be readily accessible to the person(s) responsible for the recall, and should contain sufficient information on distributors and directly supplied customers (with addresses, phone and/or fax numbers inside and outside working hours, batch numbers at least for medicinal products bearing safety features as required by legislation and quantities delivered), including those for exported products and medicinal product samples.

The progress of the recall process should be recorded for a final report.

---

[1] Article 80(i) of Directive 2001/83/EC.

Chapter 7 — Outsourced Activities

7.1 Principle

Any activity covered by the GDP guide that is outsourced should be correctly defined, agreed and controlled in order to avoid misunderstandings which could affect the integrity of the product. There must be a written contract between the contract giver and the contract acceptor which clearly establishes the duties of each party.

7.2 Contract giver

The contract giver is responsible for the activities contracted out.

The contract giver is responsible for assessing the competence of the contract acceptor to successfully carry out the work required and for ensuring by means of the contract and through audits that the principles and guidelines of GDP are followed. An audit of the contract acceptor should be performed before commencement of, and whenever there has been a change to, the outsourced activities. The frequency of audit should be defined based on risk depending on the nature of the outsourced activities. Audits should be permitted at any time.

The contract giver should provide the contract acceptor with all the information necessary to carry out the contracted operations in accordance with the specific product requirements and any other relevant requirements.

7.3 Contract acceptor

The contract acceptor should have adequate premises and equipment, procedures, knowledge and experience, and competent personnel to carry out the work ordered by the contract giver.

The contract acceptor should not pass to a third party any of the work entrusted to him under the contract without the contract giver's prior evaluation and approval of the arrangements and an audit of the third party by the contract giver or the contract acceptor. Arrangements made between the contract acceptor and any third party should ensure that the wholesale distribution information is made available in the same way as between the original contract giver and contract acceptor.

The contract acceptor should refrain from any activity which may adversely affect the quality of the product(s) handled for the contract giver.

The contract acceptor must forward any information that can influence the quality of the product(s) to the contract giver in accordance with the requirement of the contract.

Chapter 8 – Self-inspections

8.1 Principle

Self-inspections should be conducted in order to monitor implementation and compliance with GDP principles and to propose necessary corrective measures.

8.2 Self-inspections

A self-inspection programme should be implemented covering all aspects of GDP and compliance with the regulations, guidelines and procedures within a defined time frame. Self-inspections may be divided into several individual self-inspections of limited scope.

Self-inspections should be conducted in an impartial and detailed way by designated competent company personnel. Audits by independent external experts may also be useful but may not be used as a substitute for self-inspection.

All self-inspections should be recorded. Reports should contain all the observations made during the inspection. A copy of the report should be provided to the management and other relevant persons. In the event that irregularities and/or deficiencies are observed, their cause should be determined and the corrective and preventive actions (CAPA) should be documented and followed up.

Chapter 9 – Transportation

9.1 Principle

It is the responsibility of the supplying wholesale distributor to protect medicinal products against breakage, adulteration and theft, and to ensure that temperature conditions are maintained within acceptable limits during transport.

Regardless of the mode of transport, it should be possible to demonstrate that the medicines have not been exposed to conditions that may compromise their quality and integrity. A risk-based approach should be utilised when planning transportation.

9.2   Transportation

The required storage conditions for medicinal products should be maintained during transportation within the defined limits as described by the manufacturers or on the outer packaging.

If a deviation such as temperature excursion or product damage has occurred during transportation, this should be reported to the distributor and recipient of the affected medicinal products. A procedure should also be in place for investigating and handling temperature excursions.

It is the responsibility of the wholesale distributor to ensure that vehicles and equipment used to distribute, store or handle medicinal products are suitable for their use and appropriately equipped to prevent exposure of the products to conditions that could affect their quality and packaging integrity.

There should be written procedures in place for the operation and maintenance of all vehicles and equipment involved in the distribution process, including cleaning and safety precautions.

Risk assessment of delivery routes should be used to determine where temperature controls are required. Equipment used for temperature monitoring during transport within vehicles and/or containers, should be maintained and calibrated at regular intervals at least once a year.

Dedicated vehicles and equipment should be used, where possible, when handling medicinal products. Where non-dedicated vehicles and equipment are used procedures should be in place to ensure that the quality of the medicinal product will not be compromised.

Deliveries should be made to the address stated on the delivery note and into the care or the premises of the consignee. Medicinal products should not be left on alternative premises.

For emergency deliveries outside normal business hours, persons should be designated and written procedures should be available.

Where transportation is performed by a third party, the contract in place should encompass the requirements of Chapter 7. Transportation providers should be made aware by the wholesale distributor of the relevant transport conditions applicable to the consignment. Where the transportation route includes unloading and reloading or transit storage at a transportation hub, particular attention should be paid to temperature monitoring, cleanliness and the security of any intermediate storage facilities.

Provision should be made to minimise the duration of temporary storage while awaiting the next stage of the transportation route.

9.3   Containers, packaging and labelling

Medicinal products should be transported in containers that have no adverse effect on the quality of the products, and that offer adequate protection from external influences, including contamination.

Selection of a container and packaging should be based on the storage and transportation requirements of the medicinal products; the space required for the amount of medicines; the anticipated external temperature extremes; the estimated maximum time for transportation including transit storage at customs; the qualification status of the packaging and the validation status of the shipping containers.

Containers should bear labels providing sufficient information on handling and storage requirements and precautions to ensure that the products are properly handled and secured at all times. The containers should enable identification of the contents of the containers and the source.

9.4   Products requiring special conditions

In relation to deliveries containing medicinal products requiring special conditions such as narcotics or psychotropic substances, the wholesale distributor should maintain a safe and secure supply chain for these products in accordance with requirements laid down by the Member States concerned. There should be additional control systems in place for delivery of these products. There should be a protocol to address the occurrence of any theft.

Medicinal products comprising highly active and radioactive materials should be transported in safe, dedicated and secure containers and vehicles. The relevant safety measures should be in accordance with international agreements and national legislation.

For temperature-sensitive products, qualified equipment (e.g. thermal packaging, temperature-controlled containers or temperature controlled vehicles) should be used to ensure correct transport conditions are maintained between the manufacturer, wholesale distributor and customer.

If temperature-controlled vehicles are used, the temperature monitoring equipment used during transport should be maintained and calibrated at regular intervals. Temperature mapping under representative conditions should be carried out and should take into account seasonal variations.

If requested, customers should be provided with information to demonstrate that products have complied with the temperature storage conditions.

If cool packs are used in insulated boxes, they need to be located such that the product does not come in direct contact with the cool pack. Staff must be trained on the procedures for assembly of the insulated boxes (seasonal configurations) and on the re-use of cool packs.

There should be a system in place to control the re-use of cool packs to ensure that incompletely cooled packs are not used in error. There should be adequate physical segregation between frozen and chilled ice packs.

The process for delivery of sensitive products and control of seasonal temperature variations should be described in a written procedure.

Chapter 10 – Specific Provisions for Brokers[1]

10.1 Principle

A 'broker' is a person involved in activities in relation to the sale or purchase of medicinal products, except for wholesale distribution, that do not include physical handling and that consist of negotiating independently and on behalf of another legal or natural person.[2]

Brokers are subject to a registration requirement. They must have a permanent address and contact details in the Member State where they are registered[3]. They must notify the competent authority of any changes to those details without unnecessary delay.

By definition, brokers do not procure, supply or hold medicines. Therefore, requirements for premises, installations and equipment as set out in Directive 2001/83/EC do not apply. However, all other rules in Directive 2001/83/EC that apply to wholesale distributors also apply to brokers.

10.2 Quality system

The quality system of a broker should be defined in writing, approved and kept up to date. It should set out responsibilities, processes and risk management in relation to their activities.

The quality system should include an emergency plan which ensures effective recall of medicinal products from the market ordered by the manufacturer or the competent authorities or carried out in cooperation with the manufacturer or marketing authorisation holder for the medicinal product concerned[4]. The competent authorities must be immediately informed of any suspected falsified medicines offered in the supply chain[5].

---

[1] Article 85b(3) of Directive 2001/83/EC.
[2] Article 1(17a) of Directive 2001/83/EC.
[3] Article 85b of Directive 2001/83/EC.
[4] Article 80(d) of Directive 2001/83/EC.
[5] Article 85b(1), third paragraph of Directive 2001/83/EC.

10.3 Personnel

Any member of personnel involved in the brokering activities should be trained in the applicable EU and national legislation and in the issues concerning falsified medicinal products.

10.4 Documentation

The general provisions on documentation in Chapter 4 apply.

In addition, at least the following procedures and instructions, along with the corresponding records of execution, should be in place:

(i)   procedure for complaints handling;

(ii)   procedure for informing competent authorities and marketing authorisation holders of suspected falsified medicinal products;

(iii)   procedure for supporting recalls;

(iv)   procedure for ensuring that medicinal products brokered have a marketing authorisation;

(v)   procedure for verifying that their supplying wholesale distributors hold a distribution authorisation, their supplying manufacturers or importers hold a manufacturing authorisation and their customers are authorised to supply medicinal products in the Member State concerned;

(vi)   records should be kept either in the form of purchase/sales invoices or on computer, or in any other form for any transaction in medicinal products brokered and should contain at least the following information: date; name of the medicinal product; quantity brokered; name and address of the supplier and the customer; and batch number at least for products bearing the safety features.

Records should be made available to the competent authorities, for inspection purposes, for the period stated in national legislation but at least five years.

Chapter 11 — Final Provisions

These Guidelines replace the Guidelines on Good Distribution Practice of medicinal products for human use, published on 1 March 1994[1] and the Guidelines of 7 March 2013 on Good Distribution Practice of medicinal products for human use[2].

These Guidelines will be applied from the first day following their publication in the *Official Journal of the European Union*. EN C 343/12 Official Journal of the European Union 23.11.2013.

---

[1] OJ C 63, 1.3.1994, p. 4.

[2] OJ C 68, 8.3.2013, p. 1.

Glossary of terms

Term	Definition
Good Distribution Practice (GDP)	GDP is that part of quality assurance which ensures that the quality of medicinal products is maintained throughout all stages of the supply chain from the site of manufacturer to the pharmacy or person authorised or entitled to supply medicinal products to the public.
Export procedure	Export procedure: allow Community goods to leave the customs territory of the Union. For the purpose of these guidelines, the supply of medicines from EU Member State to a contracting State of the European Economic Area is not considered as export.
Falsified medicinal product[1]	Any medicinal product with a false representation of: (a) its identity, including its packaging and labelling, its name or its composition as regards any of the ingredients including excipients and the strength of those ingredients; (b) its source, including its manufacturer, its country of manufacturing, its country of origin or its marketing authorisation holder; or (c) its history, including the records and documents relating to the distribution channels used.
Free zones and free warehouses[2]	Free zones and free warehouses are parts of the customs territory of the Community or premises situated in that territory and separated from the rest of it in which: (a) Community goods are considered, for the purpose of import duties and commercial policy import measures, as not being on Community customs territory, provided they are not released for free circulation or placed under another customs procedure or used or consumed under conditions other than those provided for in customs regulations; (b) Community goods for which such provision is made under Community legislation governing specific fields qualify, by virtue of being placed in a free zone or free warehouse, for measures normally attaching to the export of goods.

(Continued)

Glossary of terms (*Continued*)

Term	Definition
Holding	Storing medicinal products.
Transport	Moving medicinal products between two locations without storing them for unjustified periods of time.
Procuring	Obtaining, acquiring, purchasing or buying medicinal products from manufacturers, importers or other wholesale distributors.
Qualification	Action of proving that any equipment works correctly and actually leads to the expected results. The word 'validation' is sometimes widened to incorporate the concept of qualification. (Defined in EudraLex Volume 4 Glossary to the GMP Guidelines).
Supplying	All activities of providing, selling, donating medicinal products to wholesalers, pharmacists, or persons authorised or entitled to supply medicinal products to the public.
Quality risk management	A systematic process for the assessment, control, communication and review of risks to the quality of the drug (medicinal) product across the product lifecycle.
Quality system	The sum of all aspects of a system that implements quality policy and ensures that quality objectives are met. (International Conference on Harmonisation of Technical Requirements for Registration of Pharmaceuticals for Human Use, Q9).
Validation	Action of proving that any procedure, process, equipment, material, activity or system actually leads to the expected results (see also 'qualification'). (Defined in EudraLex Volume 4 Glossary to the GMP Guidelines)

[1] Article 1(33) of Directive 2001/83/EC.
[2] Articles 166 to Article 181 of Council Regulation (EEC) No 2913/92 of 12 October 1992 establishing the Community Customs Code, (OJ L 302, 19.10.1992, p. 1).

UK Guidance on Wholesale Distribution Practice

Contents

The Application and Inspection Process "What to Expect"

Applicants for a new wholesale dealer's licence (WDA(H)) or existing licence holders wishing to vary their licence should apply using the MHRA Process Licensing Portal accessible via the MHRA website.[1]

MHRA acting as the licensing authority will only issue a wholesale dealer's licence when it is satisfied, following an inspection of the site(s), that the information contained in the application is accurate and in compliance with the requirements of the legislation.

When appropriate, MHRA may refuse to grant a wholesale dealer's licence or may grant a wholesale dealer's licence otherwise than as applied for. In such cases the licensing authority will notify the applicant of its proposals. The notification will set out the reasons for its proposals and give the applicant a period of not less than 28 days to respond.

Planning

Fee bearing inspections of licensed wholesale dealers are carried out to assess the degree of compliance to standards of Good Distribution Practice (GDP) and compliance with the provisions of the licence.

---

[1] http://www.mhra.gov.uk/Howweregulate/Medicines/Licensingofmedicines/Informationforlicenceapplicants/Licenceapplicationforms/Wholesaledealerslicencesapplicationforms/index.htm

Inspections of wholesaler dealers (WDA(H) holders) are undertaken as part of the risk-based inspection programme, further details of which can be found in another section of this guide.

Notification

Advance notice of inspection is normally given to a company, unless circumstances require that an unannounced inspection should take place. The timing of the inspection would normally be notified in writing by the inspector.

In accordance with the GDP risk-based inspection process, sites will be required to complete a Compliance Report in advance of inspection. Further information and guidance can be found in our risk-based inspections section.

Conduct

The major stages of the inspection process are:

- the introductory or opening meeting
- the detailed site inspection
- the summary or closing meeting

Introductory or opening meeting

The purpose of the meeting is for the Inspector to meet with the appropriate key personnel from the company to discuss the arrangements for the inspection. The Inspector would typically confirm the nature of the business, premises and security arrangements, areas to be visited and any documentation which may be required.

Site inspection

The purpose of the site inspection is to determine the degree of conformity of the operations to the requirements of Good Distribution Practice and to assess compliance with the terms and conditions of licences issued under the appropriate legislation or with details submitted in support of an application for a licence. The inspection will typically involve visits to goods receipt, storage and dispatch areas (including ambient and refrigerated), returns/quarantine area, interviews with key personnel and a review of stock movement and quality system documentation including product recalls. Any observations, recommendations and deficiencies noted during the inspection would normally be discussed with the company representatives at the time.

During inspections of manufacturing and wholesale operations, samples of starting materials, work in progress and finished products may be taken for testing if an Inspector considers that this might assist in the detection of quality deficiencies. Occasionally, samples may be taken when these cannot be obtained from other sources, for routine surveillance purposes.

Summary or closing meeting

The purpose of the meeting is for the Inspector to provide the company with a verbal summary of the inspection findings and to allow the company to correct at this stage any misconceptions. The Inspector would typically summarise the definition and classification of deficiencies they propose to report and the company are encouraged to give an undertaking to resolve the deficiencies and to agree a provisional timetable for corrective action. The Inspector would also describe the arrangements for the formal notification of the deficiencies to the company (the post-inspection letter) and what is expected as a response.

Deficiencies are classified as follows:

- *Critical deficiency:*

Any departure from Guidelines on Good Distribution Practice resulting in a medicinal product causing a significant risk to the patient and public health. This includes an activity increasing the risk of falsified medicines reaching the patients. A combination of a number of major deficiencies that indicates a serious systems failure. An example of a critical deficiency could be:

Purchase from or supply of medicinal products to a non-authorised person; Storage of products requiring refrigeration at ambient temperatures; Rejected or recalled products found in sellable stock.

- *Major Deficiency:*

A non-critical deficiency: which indicates a major deviation from Good Distribution Practice; **or** which has caused or may cause a medicinal product not to comply with its marketing authorisation in particular its storage and transport conditions; **or** which indicates a major deviation from the terms and provisions of the wholesale distribution authorisation; **or** a combination of several other deficiencies, none of which on their own may be major, but which may together represent a major deficiency.

● *Other Deficiency*:

A deficiency which cannot be classified as either critical or major, but which indicates a departure from Guidelines on Good Distribution Practice.

The choice of company representatives at the meeting is primarily for the company to decide, but should normally include the senior staff who were present during the inspection and the Responsible Person (RP).

Depending upon the inspection findings and the response from the company during and following the inspection, the Inspector may take one of a number of actions ranging from:

- issuing a GDP certificate confirming essential compliance with GDP
- referral to the Compliance escalation process or the Inspection Action Group (IAG) for consideration for adverse licensing action where serious non-compliance is found.

Further information on the Compliance escalation process and IAG can be found in this publication.

Company responses

The inspected site is expected to provide a written response (by letter or email) to the post-inspection letter within the required timeframe. The response should consider the context of the deficiency within the overall quality system rather than just the specific issue identified. The response should include proposals for dealing with the deficiencies, together with a timetable for their implementation. The response should be structured as follows:

- Restate the deficiency number and the deficiency as written below.
- State the proposed corrective action.
- State the proposed target date for the completion of the corrective action(s).
- Include any comment the company considers appropriate.
- Provide evidence supporting any corrective action where it is considered appropriate.

Inspection report

Once the Inspector is satisfied that any necessary remedial action has been taken or is in hand and that the site is essentially in compliance with GDP, an inspection report and GDP certificate are finalised.

Risk-based Inspection Programme

Introduction

MHRA has been incorporating elements of risk management into its inspection programme for a number of years. A formal risk-based inspection (RBI) programme was implemented on 1 April 2009, following public consultation MLX 345. The RBI programme covers all aspects of good practices associated with the inspection of clinical, pre-clinical and quality control laboratories, clinical trials, manufacturers, wholesalers and pharmacovigilance systems. The primary aim of the RBI programme is to enable inspectorate resources to focus on areas that maximise protection of public health while reducing the overall administrative and economic burden to stakeholders.

Sentinel risk information module

Working with technology partners Accenture, MHRA established its Sentinel IT system in 2005 which is used by most agency business areas to manage business processes for:

- marketing authorisations
- pharmacovigilance
- clinical trials
- manufacturer's and wholesale dealer's licences
- inspections
- issuing GMP and GDP certificates and automatic loading of these into the EMA's EudraGMDP database.

In February 2013 a newly developed Sentinel risk information module was deployed to expand upon the paper-based RBI system initiated in 2009.

The Risk Estimation Tool uses the intelligence data collected on regulated companies, their respective sites and previous inspection results across all GxP areas to predict a risk score as "likely next inspection result". This score is calculated for every site and can be interpreted as a weighted sum of inspection findings. Companies/sites are ranked based on predicted risk and business rules are applied to suggest a next inspection date.

A planning step allows inspectors to accept or reject the suggested date taking into account other information which may not be included in the statistical calculation. For estimation of the risk score, the tool uses a logistic regression statistical model incorporating all data elements for all companies and sites. The model is fit (i.e. recomputed) monthly based on the most recent data extracted from Sentinel. The Empirica algorithm software was designed by Oracle Health Services to provide detailed analysis of the risk information. MHRA first used Empirica software in 2006 for pharmacovigilance signal detection and management.

The model estimates the association between inspection findings and other covariates (events) observed in data. The algorithm makes a global estimate on how these events affect inspection score within a GxP and then applies this when these events are recorded in the future. As a result those factors which are statistically most relevant to risk will receive the highest weighting and this will be continuously updated as more events are recorded. The model looks at events over a five year period but applies greater significance to more recent data.

Current implementation status

A number of aspects of the algorithm are being validated including;

- The risk score
- The weighting of inspection outcomes
- The weighting of the risk events
- The generation of proposed inspection dates from the risk score
- Inclusion of all appropriate risk events

The algorithm is being assessed on an individual GxP basis as well as across the GxPs. The algorithm output is being compared against the existing RBI processes within the GxPs. Until the algorithm has been successfully validated the existing risk-based inspection scheduling processes will remain in place.

GDP risk-based inspection (RBI) programme

The GDP risk-based inspection process commenced for all wholesale dealer's licence holders on 1 April 2009.

Compliance report

Sites will be required to complete a Compliance Report in advance of inspection, this will be prompted by the inspector. Guidance to completing the report can be found within the document. The Compliance Report should be returned to your inspector prior to the inspection.

Risk rating process

Inspectors use the inspection outputs along with a number of other factors to identify a risk rating for the site, which equates to a future inspection frequency. As this process is not concluded until the inspection is closed the risk ratings **will not** be discussed at the closing meetings. However a copy of the full inspection report which includes the full risk rating rationale is provided to sites once the inspection has been closed.

Issue of a certificate of GDP compliance and/or support of the site on the relevant licence is indication of meeting the minimum level of GDP compliance. Risk ratings identify the degree of surveillance required within the licensing and inspection program. There is no intention that sites be rated against each other as a result of risk ratings assigned by MHRA. Risk ratings can change following inspection resulting in either increased or decreased risk. Inspection risk ratings will not be published by MHRA.

There will be no formal process of appeal against risk ratings and future inspection frequency. However any rating that results in an increased inspection frequency from the previous standard will be peer reviewed before conclusion by a GDP operations manager. MHRA does have a formal complaints process if sites wish to log an issue, however any concerns regarding the inspection process should be raised with the inspector.

Conditions of Holding a Wholesale Dealer's Licence

The holder of a wholesale dealer's licence must comply with certain conditions in relation to the wholesale distribution of medicinal products. These conditions are set out in regulations 43 – 45 of the Human Medicines Regulations 2012 [SI 2012/1916] ("the Regulations"). They require that the licence holder shall:

- comply with the guidelines on Good Distribution Practice (GDP);[1]
- ensure, within the limits of their responsibility as a distributor of medicinal products, the appropriate and continued supply of such medicinal products to pharmacies and persons who may lawfully sell such products by retail or who may lawfully supply them in circumstances corresponding to retail sale, so that the needs of patients in the UK are met;
- provide and maintain such staff, premises, equipment and facilities for the handling, storage and distribution of the medicinal products under the licence as are necessary to maintain the quality of, and ensure proper distribution of the medicinal products;
- inform the licensing authority of any proposed structural alteration to, or discontinued use of, premises to which the licence relates or premises which have been approved by the licensing authority;
- inform the licensing authority of any change to the Responsible Person;

---

[1] Guidelines on Good Distribution Practice of Medicinal Products for Human Use (2013/C 343/01) http://eur-lex.europa.eu/LexUriServ/LexUriServ.do?uri=OJ:C:2013:343:0001:0014:EN:PDF.

- not sell or offer for sale or supply any medicinal product unless there is a marketing authorisation, Article 126a authorisation, certificate of registration or traditional herbal registration ("an authorisation") for the time being in force in respect of that product; and the sale or offer for sale is in accordance with the provisions of that authorisation. This restriction on the holder of a wholesale dealer's licence shall not apply to:
  - the sale or offer for sale of a special medicinal product; and
  - the export to an EEA State, or supply for the purposes of such export, of a medicinal product which may be placed on the market in that State without a marketing authorisation, Article 126a authorisation, certificate of registration or traditional herbal registration by virtue of legislation adopted by that State under Article 5(1) of the 2001 Directive; or
  - the sale or supply, or offer for sale or supply, of an unauthorised medicinal product where the Secretary of State has temporarily authorised the distribution of the product under regulation 174 of the Regulations.

The holder of a wholesale dealer's licence shall:

- keep such documents relating to the sale of medicinal products to which their licence relates as will facilitate the withdrawal or recall from sale of medicinal products in accordance with an emergency plan referred to below;
- have in place an emergency plan which will ensure effective implementation of the recall from the market of any relevant medicinal products where such recall is:
  - ordered by the licensing authority or by the competent authority of any other EEA State, or
  - carried out in co-operation with the manufacturer of, or the holder of the marketing authorisation for, the product in question;
- keep records in relation to the receipt, dispatch or brokering of medicinal products, of the date of receipt, the date of despatch, the date of brokering, the name of the medicinal product, the quantity of the product received, dispatched or brokered, the name and address of the person from whom the products were received or to whom they are dispatched, and the batch number of medicinal products bearing safety features referred to in point (o) of Article 54 of the 2001 Directive.[2]

Where the holder of a wholesale dealer's licence imports from another EEA State for which they are not the holder of the marketing authorisation, Article 126a authorisation, certificate of registration or a traditional herbal registration of the product, then they shall notify the holder of that

---

[2] Point (o) of Article 54 was inserted by Directive 2011/62/EU of the European Parliament and of the Council (OJ No L 174, 1.7.2011, p74).

authorisation of their intention to import that product. In the case where the product is the subject of a marketing authorisation granted under Regulation (EC) No 726/2004, the holder of the wholesale dealer's licence shall notify the EMA or for any other authorisation they shall notify the licensing authority. In both cases they will be required to pay a fee to the EMA in accordance with Article 76(4) of the 2001 Directive[3] or the licensing authority as the case may be, in accordance with the Fees Regulations. These requirements will not apply in relation to the wholesale distribution of medicinal products to a person in a non-EEA country.

The licence holder, for the purposes of enabling the licensing authority to determine whether there are grounds for suspending, revoking or varying the licence, must permit a person authorised in writing by the licensing authority, on production of identification, to carry out any inspection, or to take any samples or copies, which an inspector could carry out or take under Part 16 (enforcement) of the Regulations.

The holder of a wholesale dealer's licence must verify that any medicinal products they receive which are required by Article 54a of the Directive[4] to bear safety features are not falsified. This does not apply in relation to the distribution of medicinal products received from a third country by a person for supply to a person in a third country. Any verification is carried out by checking the safety features on the outer packaging, in accordance with the requirements laid down in the delegated acts adopted under Article 54a(2) of the 2001 Directive.

The licence holder must maintain a quality system setting out responsibilities, processes and risk management measures in relation to their activities.

The licence holder must also immediately inform the licensing authority and, where applicable, the marketing authorisation holder, of medicinal products which the licence holder receives or is offered which the licence holder knows or suspects, or has reasonable grounds for knowing or suspecting, to be falsified.

Where the medicinal product is obtained through brokering, the licence holder must verify that the broker involved fulfils the requirements set out in the Regulations.

The licence holder must not obtain supplies of medicinal products from anyone except the holder of a manufacturer's licence or wholesale dealer's licence in relation to products of that description or the person who holds an authorisation granted by another EEA State authorising the manufacture of products of the description or their distribution by way of wholesale dealing. The supply must be in accordance with the principles

---

[3] Article 76(4) was inserted by Directive 2011/62/EU of the European Parliament and of the Council (OJ No L 174, 1.7.2011, p74).

[4] Article 54a was inserted by Directive 2011/62/EU of the European Parliament and of the Council (OJ No L 174, 1.7.2011, p74).

and guidelines of good distribution practice. This does not apply in relation to the distribution of medicinal products directly received from a non-EEA country but not imported into the EU.

From 28th October 2013, where the medicinal product is directly received from a non-EEA country for export to a non-EEA country, the licensed wholesale dealer must check that the supplier of the medicinal product in the exporting non-EEA country is authorised or entitled to supply such medicinal products in accordance with the legal and administrative provisions in that country.

The holder of a wholesale dealer's licence must verify that the wholesale dealer who supplies the product complies with the principles and guidelines of good distribution practices; or the manufacturer or importer who supplies the product holds a manufacturing authorisation.

The holder of a wholesale dealer's licence may distribute medicinal products by way of wholesale dealing only to the holder of a wholesale dealer's licence relating to those products, the holder of an authorisation granted by the competent authority of another EEA State authorising the supply of those products by way of wholesale dealing, a person who may lawfully sell those products by retail or may lawfully supply them in circumstances corresponding to retail sale; or a person who may lawfully administer those products. This does not apply in relation to medicinal products which are distributed by way of wholesale dealing to a person in a non-EEA country.

From 28th October 2013, where the medicinal product is supplied directly to persons in a non-EEA country the licensed wholesale dealer must check that the person that receives it is authorised or entitled to receive medicinal products for wholesale distribution or supply to the public in accordance with the applicable legal and administrative provisions of the non-EEA country concerned.

Where any medicinal product is supplied to any person who may lawfully sell those products by retail or who may lawfully supply them in circumstances corresponding to retail sale, the licence holder shall enclose with the product a document which makes it possible to ascertain:

- the date on which the supply took place;
- the name and pharmaceutical form of the product supplied;
- the quantity of product supplied;
- the names and addresses of the person or persons from whom the products were supplied to the licence holder; and
- the batch number of the medicinal products bearing the safety features referred to in point (o) of Article 54 of the 2001 Directive.

The holder of a wholesale dealer's licence shall keep a record of the information supplied where any medicinal product is supplied to any person who may lawfully sell those products by retail or who may lawfully supply them in circumstance corresponding to retail sale for a minimum period of five years after the date on which it is supplied and ensure, during that period, that that record is available to the licensing authority for inspection.

The wholesale dealer's licence holder shall at all times have at their disposal the services of a responsible person who, in the opinion of the licensing authority has knowledge of the activities to be carried out and of the procedures to be performed under the licence which is adequate for performing the functions of responsible person; and has experience in those procedures and activities which is adequate for those purposes.

The functions of the responsible person shall be to ensure, in relation to medicinal products, that the conditions under which the licence has been granted have been, and are being, complied with and the quality of medicinal products which are being handled by the wholesale dealer's licence holder are being maintained in accordance with the requirements of the marketing authorisations, Article 126a authorisations, certificates of registration or traditional herbal registrations applicable to those products.

The standard provisions for wholesale dealer's licences, that is, those provisions which may be included in all licences unless the licence specifically provides otherwise, insofar as those licences relate to relevant medicinal products, shall be those provisions set out in Part 4 of Schedule 4 of the Regulations.

The licence holder shall not use any premises for the purpose of the handling, storage or distribution of relevant medicinal products other than those specified in their licence or notified to the licensing authority by them and approved by the licensing authority.

The licence holder shall provide such information as may be requested by the licensing authority concerning the type and quantity of any relevant medicinal products which they handle, store or distribute.

Where and insofar as the licence relates to special medicinal products to which regulation 167 of the Regulations apply which do not have a UK or EMA authorisation and are commonly known as "specials" (refer to Guidance Note 14), the licence holder shall only import such products from another EEA State in response to an order which satisfies the requirements of regulation 167 of the Regulations; and where the following conditions are complied with:

- No later than 28 days prior to each importation of a special medicinal product, the licence holder shall give written notice to the licensing authority stating their intention to import that special medicinal product and stating the following particulars:
  - the name of the medicinal product, being the brand name or the common name, or the scientific name, and any name, if different, under which the medicinal product is to be sold or supplied in the United Kingdom;
  - any trademark or name of the manufacturer of the medicinal product,

- – in respect of each active constituent of the medicinal product, any international non-proprietary name or the British approved name or the monograph name or, where that constituent does not have an international non-proprietary name, a British approved name or a monograph name, the accepted scientific name or any other name descriptive of the true nature of that constituent,
- – the quantity of medicinal product which is to be imported which shall not exceed more, on any one occasion, than such amount as is sufficient for 25 single administrations, or for 25 courses of treatment where the amount imported is sufficient for a maximum of three months' treatment, and
- – the name and address of the manufacturer or assembler of that medicinal product in the form in which it is to be imported and, if the person who will supply that medicinal product for importation is not the manufacturer or assembler, the name and address of such supplier.

- Subject to the next bullet point below, the licence holder shall not import the special medicinal product if, before the end of 28 days from the date on which the licensing authority sends or gives the licence holder an acknowledgement in writing by the licensing authority that they have received the notice referred to in the bullet point above, the licensing authority have notified them in writing that the product should not be imported.
- The licence holder may import the special medicinal product referred to in the notice where they have been notified in writing by the licensing authority, before the end of the 28 day period referred to in the bullet point above, that the special medicinal product may be imported.
- Where the licence holder sells or supplies special medicinal products, they shall, in addition to any other records which they are required to make by the provisions of their licence, make and maintain written records relating to the batch number of the batch of the product from which the sale or supply was made and details of any adverse reaction to the product so sold or supplied of which they become aware.
- The licence holder shall import no more on any one occasion than such amount as is sufficient for 25 single administrations, or for 25 courses of treatment where the amount imported is sufficient for a maximum of three months' treatment, and on any such occasion shall not import more than the quantity notified to the licensing authority in the notification of intention to import.
- The licence holder shall inform the licensing authority forthwith of any matter coming to their attention which might reasonably cause the licensing authority to believe that the medicinal product can no longer be regarded either as a product which can safely be administered to human beings or as a product which is of satisfactory quality for such administration.

- The licence holder shall not issue any advertisement, catalogue or circular relating to the special medicinal product or make any representations in respect of that product.
- The licence holder shall cease importing or supplying a special medicinal product if they have received a notice in writing from the licensing authority directing that, as from a date specified in that notice, a particular product or class of products shall no longer be imported or supplied.

The licence holder shall take all reasonable precautions and exercise all due diligence to ensure that any information they provide to the licensing authority which is relevant to an evaluation of the safety, quality or efficacy of any medicinal product for human use which they handle, store or distribute is not false or misleading in a material particular.

Where a wholesale dealer's licence relates to exempt advanced therapy medicinal products the licence holder shall keep the data for the system for the traceability of the advanced therapy medicinal products for such period, being a period of longer than 30 years, as may be specified by the licensing authority.

The Standard Provisions also require the holder of a wholesale dealer's licence that relates to exempt advanced therapy medicinal products to obtain supplies of exempt advanced therapy medicinal products only from the holder of a manufacturer's licence in respect of those products or the holder of a wholesale dealer's licence in respect of those products.

The licence holder must:

- distribute an exempt advanced therapy medicinal product by way of wholesale dealing only to the holder of a wholesale dealer's licence in respect of those products; or a person who may lawfully administer those products, and solicited the product for an individual patient;
- establish and maintain a system ensuring that the exempt advanced therapy medicinal product and its starting and raw materials, including all substances coming into contact with the cells or tissues it may contain, can be traced through the sourcing, manufacturing, packaging, storage, transport and delivery to the establishment where the product is used;
- inform the licensing authority of any adverse reaction to any exempt advanced therapy medicinal product supplied by the holder of the wholesale dealer's licence of which the holder is aware;
- keep the data for ensuring traceability for a minimum of 30 years after the expiry date of the exempt advanced therapy medicinal product or longer as specified by the licensing authority;
- ensure that the data for ensuring traceability will, in the event that the licence is suspended, revoked or withdrawn or the licence holder becomes bankrupt or insolvent, be held available to the licensing authority by the holder of a wholesale dealer's licence for the same period that the data has to be kept; and
- not import or export any exempt advanced therapy medicinal product.

Appointment and Duties of the Responsible Person

Title VII of the Directive on the Community code relating to medicinal products for human use (Directive 2001/83/EC) obliges holders of a distribution authorisation to have a "qualified person designated as responsible". Regulation 45 of the Human Medicines Regulations 2012 [SI 2012/1916] state the requirement for a Responsible Person (RP) within the UK.

The RP is responsible for safeguarding product users against potential hazards arising from poor distribution practices as a result, for example, of purchasing suspect products, poor storage or failure to establish the bona fides of purchasers. The duties of a RP include:

- to ensure that the provisions of the licence are observed
- to ensure that the guidelines on Good Distribution Practice (GDP) are complied with
- to ensure that the operations do not compromise the quality of medicines
- to ensure that an adequate quality system is established and maintained
- to oversee audit of the quality system and to carry out independent audits
- to ensure that adequate records are maintained
- to ensure that all personnel are trained
- to ensure full and prompt cooperation with marketing authorisation holders in the event of recalls.

In order to carry out his duties, the RP should be resident in the UK and have a clear reporting line to the licence holder or MD. The RP should have personal knowledge of the products traded under the licence and the conditions necessary for their safe storage and distribution. The RP should have access to all areas, sites, stores and records which relate to the licensable activities and regularly review and monitor all such areas, etc. and the standards achieved.

If the RP is not adequately carrying out those duties, the licensing authority may consider the suspension of the licence, withdrawal of acceptance of the RP on that licence and the acceptability on any other licence.

The RP does not have to be an employee of the licence holder but must be available to the licence holder when required. Where the RP is not an employee, there should be a written contract specifying responsibilities, duties, authority and so on.

In the case of small companies, the licensing authority may accept the licence holder as the nominated RP. In larger companies, however, this is not desirable.

There is no statutory requirement for the RP to be a pharmacist.

The RP should have access to pharmaceutical knowledge and advice when it is required, and have personal knowledge of:

- The relevant provisions of the Human Medicines Regulations 2012 [SI 2012/1916].
- Directive 2001/83/EC as amended on the wholesale distribution of medicinal products for human use.
- The EU Guidelines on Good Distribution Practice of Medicinal Products for Human Use (2013/C 343/01).
- The conditions of the wholesale dealer's licence for which nominated.
- The products traded under the licence and the conditions necessary for their safe storage and distribution.
- The categories of persons to whom products may be distributed.

Where the RP is not a pharmacist or eligible to act as a Qualified Person (QP) (as defined in Directive 2001/83/EC as amended), the RP should have at least one year's practical experience in both or either of the following areas:

- Handling, storage and distribution of medicinal products.
- Transactions in or selling or procuring medicinal products.
  In addition, the RP should have at least one year's managerial experience in controlling and directing the wholesale distribution of medicinal products on a scale, and of a kind, appropriate to the licence for which nominated.

  To carry out responsibilities, the RP should:

- Have a clear reporting line to either the licence holder or the Managing Director.
- Have access to all areas, sites, stores, staff and records relating to the licensable activities being carried out.
- Demonstrate regular review and monitoring of all such areas, sites and staff etc. or have delegated arrangements whereby the RP receives written reports that such delegated actions have been carried out on behalf of the RP in compliance with standard operating procedures and GDP.
  Where arrangements are delegated, the RP remains responsible and should personally carry out the delegated functions at least once a year.
- Focus on the management of licensable activities, the accuracy and quality of records, compliance with standard operating procedures and GDP, the quality of handling and storage equipment and facilities, and the standards achieved.
- Keep appropriate records relating to the discharge of the RP responsibilities.

Where the licence covers a number of sites, the RP may have a nominated deputy with appropriate reporting and delegating arrangements. However, the RP should be able to demonstrate to the licensing authority that the necessary controls and checks are in place.

The licence holder should ensure that there is a written standard operating procedure for receiving advice and comment from the RP and recording the consequent action taken as may be necessary.

Should it prove impossible to resolve a disagreement between the licence holder and the RP, the licensing authority should be consulted.

Whilst a joint referral is clearly to be preferred, either party may approach the licensing authority independently. If an RP finds difficulty over performing statutory responsibilities or the activities being carried out under the licence, the licensing authority should be consulted in strict confidence.

The Responsible Person Gold Standard

The Human Medicines Regulations 2012 require holders of a wholesale dealer's licence to designate and ensure that there is available at all times at least one person, referred to in the regulations as the "responsible person", who in the opinion of the licensing authority:

(a) has knowledge of the activities to be carried out and of the procedures to be performed under the licence; and

(b) has adequate experience relating to those activities and procedures.

Guidance on the role and responsibilities of the Responsible Person (RP) is set out in Chapter 2 of the EU Good Distribution Practice Guide and these remain the same irrespective of whether the RP is a permanent or contracted employee of a company.

The RP plays a vital part in ensuring the quality and the integrity of medicinal products are maintained throughout the distribution chain and it is essential that they have the right knowledge, demonstrate competence and deploy the right skills so that patients and healthcare professionals have the confidence and trust to use medicines.

In order to facilitate this and to standardise the requirements for individuals operating as, or aspiring to be, a RP, Cogent (the national skills body for the science industries) has, following extensive discussion with pharmaceutical companies and MHRA, published a new Gold Standard role profile for the RP[1].

This sets out an industry-agreed framework that identifies the skills required in four competency areas and includes not only traditional qualifications and technical requirements but also the behavioural skills necessary to do the job to a high standard.

UK GUIDANCE ON WHOLESALE DISTRIBUTION PRACTICE

---

[1] http://www.mhra.gov.uk/Howweregulate/Medicines/Inspectionandstandards/GoodManufacturingPractice/News/CON421310.

Responsible Person
Medicinal Products

The Human Medicines Regulations require a distributor to designate a Responsible Person(s), named on the applicable licence. Regulation 45 and the EU GDP Guide set out the requirements and the responsibilities.

Where the RP is contracted to a company, the duties remain the same as for those of the permanently employed RP. The responsibilities should be covered in a contract.

Compliance	**The Gold Standard** Job Role skills, knowledge and behaviours
	the individual should understand: • the role of MHRA in the licensing of medicines and as the competent authority including the risk-based inspection process, the role of the enforcement group, the Inspection Action Group (IAG), and resulting actions that can be taken due to non-compliance • the UK regulations in relation to Wholesale Distribution • the European Pharmaceutical Directive related to Wholesale Distribution of Medicinal Products • Good Distribution Practice (GDP) • the importance of a clear reporting line to the wholesale distribution authorisation holder, senior manager and/or CEO the individual shall: • employ due diligence in the discharge of their duties, maintaining full compliance to procedures and appropriate regulations • report to senior management, the Marketing Authorisation holder and the MHRA any suspicious events of which they become aware in addition, the individual also has knowledge of: • the role of the professional bodies and organisations that regulate those supplying medicinal products to the public e.g. GPhC • the role of the Home Office in relation to the handling of Controlled Drugs • the role of the Veterinary Medicines Directorate (VMD) in relation to veterinary medicines • the role of the European Medicines Agency (EMA) and use of EUDRAGMDP • the Falsified Medicines Directive • the Principles and Guidelines of Good Manufacturing Practice and how the principles of GDP maintain product quality throughout the distribution chain
Knowledge	**The Gold Standard** Job Role skills, knowledge and behaviours
	the individual should have: • the prior relevant knowledge and experience related to the distribution of medicinal products • access to pharmaceutical knowledge and advice when it is required • knowledge of the products traded under the licence • if not a pharmacist or QP, one year's relevant practical and managerial experience of medicinal products

Supported by MHRA

Responsible Person
Medicinal Products

Technical Competence	**The Gold Standard** Job Role skills, knowledge and behaviours
	the individual is able to perform duties including: **Quality Management** *the individual shall ensure that a quality management system proportionate to the distributor's activities is implemented and maintained including:* • *Quality Risk Management* • *Corrective and Preventative Actions (CAPA) to address deviations* • *Change Control* • *Measurement of performance indicators and management review* **Personnel** *The Responsible Person is required to:* • *understand their own responsibilities* • *carry out all duties in such a way as to ensure that the wholesale distributor can demonstrate GDP compliance* • *define personal and staff roles, responsibilities and accountabilities and record all delegated duties* • *ensure that initial and continuous training programmes are implemented and maintained* • *ensure all personnel are trained in GDP, their own duties, product identification, the risks of falsified medicines and specific training for products requiring more stringent handling* • *maintain training records for self and others and ensure training is periodically assessed* **Premises & Equipment** • *ensure that appropriate standards of GDP are maintained for own premises and contracted storage premises* • *identify medicinal products, legal categories, storage conditions and different Marketing Authorisation types* • *maintain the safety and security of medicinal products within the appropriate environments, including product integrity and product storage* • *use the appropriate systems to segregate, store and distribute medicinal products* • *maintain records for the repair, maintenance, calibration and validation of equipment including computerised systems* • *ensure storage areas are temperature mapped, qualified and validated* **Documentation** *The individual shall focus on:* • *the accuracy and quality of records* • *contemporaneous records* • *records storage* • *maintaining comprehensive written procedures that are understood and followed* • *ensure procedures are valid and version controlled*

Supported by MHRA　　　

UK GUIDANCE ON WHOLESALE DISTRIBUTION PRACTICE

Responsible Person
Medicinal Products

Operations
- carry out due diligence checks and ensure that suppliers and customers are qualified
- ensure all necessary checks are carried out and that medicinal products are authorised for sale
- manage authorised activities to ensure operations do not compromise the quality of medicines and can demonstrate compliance with GDP
- demonstrate the application of activities and provisions in accordance with the wholesale distribution authorisation and of company processes and procedures
- ensure that any additional requirements imposed on certain products by national law are adhered to e.g. specials, unlicensed imports & Controlled Drugs

Complaints, returns, suspected falsified medicinal products and medicinal product recalls
- ensure relevant customer complaints are dealt with effectively, informing the manufacturer and/or marketing authorisation holder of any product quality/product defect issues
- decide on the final disposition of returned, rejected, recalled or falsified products
- approve any returns to saleable stock
- coordinate and promptly perform any recall operations for medicinal products
- co-operate with marketing authorisation holders and national competent authorities in the event of recalls
- have an awareness of the issues surrounding falsified medicines

Outsourced Activities
- approve any subcontracted activities which may impact on GDP

Self-Inspection
- ensure that self-inspections are performed at appropriate regular intervals following a prearranged programme and necessary corrective measures are put in place

Transportation
- apply the appropriate transport requirements and methods for cold chain, ambient and hazardous product
- ensure all transport equipment is appropriately qualified

Brokers
- ensure that transactions are only made with brokers who are registered
- ensure that any broker activities performed are registered

Business Improvement	**The Gold Standard** Job Role skills, knowledge and behaviours
	the individual should: - practise continuous improvement practices and utilise appropriate tools and techniques to solve problems

Supported by MHRA

Responsible Person
Medicinal Products

Functional & Behavioural	**The Gold Standard** Job Role skills, knowledge and behaviours
	the individual has: <ul><li>*relevant skills in:*<ul><li>*English (level 2)*</li><li>*Mathematics (level 2)*</li><li>*ICT*</li></ul></li></ul>*the individual can demonstrate relevant personal qualities in:* *Autonomy*<ul><li>*take responsibility for planning and developing courses of action, including responsibility for the work of others*</li><li>*exercise autonomy and judgement within broad but generally well-defined parameters*</li></ul><ul><li>*Management & Leadership*<ul><li>*develop and implement operational plans for their area of responsibility*</li><li>*manage diversity & discrimination issues*</li><li>*provide leadership for their team*</li></ul></li></ul><ul><li>*Working with others*<ul><li>*ensure effective delegation whilst retaining ownership of the outcome*</li><li>*develop and maintain productive working relationships with colleagues and stakeholders*</li><li>*monitor the progress and quality of work within their area of responsibility*</li></ul></li></ul><ul><li>*Personal development*<ul><li>*manage their professional development by setting targets and planning how they will be met*</li><li>*review progress towards targets and establish evidence of achievements*</li></ul></li></ul><ul><li>*Communication*<ul><li>*put across ideas in clear and concise manner and present a well-structured case*</li><li>*communicate complex information to others*</li></ul></li></ul><ul><li>*Business*<ul><li>*understands the business environment in which the company operates*</li><li>*has an appreciation of the industry sector and competitors*</li></ul></li></ul><ul><li>*Customers*<ul><li>*understands the customer base and is aware of customer requirements*</li></ul></li></ul>

For more information on how to achieve the Gold Standard contact us on 0845 607 014

Version 2 July 2014

Supported by MHRA

UK Guidance on EU Guide Chapter 1 – Quality Management

Quality Management

A consistent focus on quality is of prime importance for all wholesale distributors in order to maintain an effective and efficient business that meets customer needs and ensures product quality is maintained.

Quality management is as much a mind-set as an activity in itself, with the aim of achieving quality processes that permeate throughout all distribution activities, with the ultimate goal of ensuring patient safety.

Quality System

The quality system is the vehicle by which quality management is delivered and it should be all encompassing. However, this doesn't mean that it has to be complicated with its size and complexity being proportionate to the distribution activities being undertaken.

Chapter 1 of the EC Guide on Good Distribution Practice (GDP) gives a detailed breakdown of the areas that should be covered.

Quality Risk Management (QRM)

QRM is not new to wholesale distributors, as informal systems have always been in place as a matter of routine. However GDP now require that the process be documented.

QRM is essentially the identification and control of risks to product quality through the evaluation of the activities that are being performed.

Underpinning this is that the evaluation of the risk is based on knowledge and experience of the process and ultimately links to the protection of the patient.

The level of effort, formality and documentation of the process should be commensurate with the level of risk.

GDP refers to ICH Q9 as a useful guidance document on QRM. This includes the principles and concepts of QRM with Annex 1 & 2 identifying various tools and techniques; www.ich.org

Change control

Change control is a formal process whereby changes to a process are identified, planned and introduced in a controlled way.

A typical change control process may consist of several stages;

● Submission of a documented change control request to management.

- Consideration and evaluation of the request by management. This evaluation should consider if the change poses any risks to public health or if there are any impacts on other processes and procedures. Actions identified at this stage should be resolved prior to approval.
- Implementation of the change.
  This is a live process and unforeseen events during implementation should be subject to a further assessment of risk,
- Review of Effectiveness. After an appropriate period an objective review of the effectiveness of the change should take place. This should consider both successes as well as any problems that have arisen, with any lessons learnt being used to improve the process for future changes.

Deviation management and Corrective and Preventative Actions (CAPA)

Distributors should prepare for circumstances when things go wrong.

When this occurs the identification of control measures should be a priority, particularly where an unplanned event may have (or has had) a significant impact on public health.

Depending on the severity of the event, there may be a process of ongoing control, requiring initial corrective actions to deal with the immediate fallout from the event through to the identification of the root cause of the problem and proactive preventative actions to avoid reoccurrence.

During investigations it is very important that the root cause of the problem is identified, as what may initially be deemed as for example, "operator error" may actually be attributable to system weaknesses elsewhere.

Corrective and Preventative actions (CAPA), are an integral part of the change control and deviation management processes; reducing the likelihood or severity of a risk event and creating an opportunity to improve and reduce the likelihood of the deviation occurring again.

Corrective actions are identified <u>after</u> a deviation with preventative actions being identified following an event and <u>before</u> a change is implemented.

Management review and monitoring

To ensure the effectiveness and continual improvement of the quality management system, there should be a process in place for regular management review.

This review should actively involve company management and key personnel such as the Responsible Person.

In very small organisations the process of review may require taking a step back and objectively reviewing the operational activities and supporting procedures.

Questions to be considered during the management review may include:

- Is the quality system effective, does it reflect the current business model?
- Are activities being carried out in accordance with the principles of Quality Management, or are there opportunities for improvement with some processes requiring modification?
- Has the regulatory landscape changed? Has legislation been amended or guidance published which means that activities need to be reviewed?
- Is the business operating effectively, are the right products getting to the right customers at the right time? What improvements can be made to address customer complaints?
- If third parties are contracted to provide services, are they complying with their contractual obligations?
- Have there been any unforeseen problems or events and has effective CAPA been implemented?
- Have planned changes been effective?
- Are there staff training or staff re-training issues?

The outcome of each management review should be documented, result in a CAPA plan where necessary and should be effectively communicated to staff.

Controls on Certain Medicinal Products

Products containing Ephedrine and Pseudoephedrine

The Drug Licensing and Compliance Unit at the Home Office is informing exporters of pseudoephedrine and ephedrine (both for human or veterinary use) outside of the European Union of amendments to the existing Drug Precursor Chemical Regulations which came into effect on the 30 December 2013. A summary of the key changes can be found on GOV. UK[1].

Drugs useable in execution by lethal injection

In December 2011, the European Union adopted a new EU-wide control on the export of certain drugs usable in execution by lethal injection.

These controls which came into force on 21 December 2011 were adopted as an amendment to Annex III of Council Regulation (EC) 1236/2005 concerning trade in certain goods which could be used for

---

[1] https://www.gov.uk/government/uploads/system/uploads/attachment_data/file/275027/precursor_regulations_changes_dec_2013.pdf

capital punishment, torture or other cruel, inhuman or degrading treatment or punishment.

You can download the full text of Council Regulation (EU) No 1352/2011 from the Eudralex website[2].

As a result of these EU imposed controls, exporters need to seek appropriate permission from national export control authorities to export to any destination outside the EU, short and intermediate acting barbiturate anaesthetic agents including, but not limited to, the following:

- amobarbital (CAS RN 57-43-2)
- amobarbital sodium salt (CAS RN 64-43-7)
- pentobarbital (CAS RN 76-74-4)
- pentobarbital sodium salt (CAS 57-33-0)
- secobarbital (CAS RN 76-73-3)
- secobarbital sodium salt (CAS RN 309-43-3)
- thiopental (CAS RN 76-75-5)
- thiopental sodium salt (CAS RN 71-73-8), also known as thiopentone sodium

The control also applies to products containing one or more of the above. These controls are intended to apply to finished products – in other words, those that are packaged for human or veterinary use. It is not intended that they should apply to raw materials or to intermediate products (ie products that require further processing to make them suitable for human or veterinary use).

The relevant national export licensing authority responsible for administering these controls in the UK is the Export Control Organisation (ECO), part of the Department for Business, Innovation and Skills (BIS). The ECO is responsible for licensing items that are judged to be of a 'strategic' nature, including goods used in torture.

Further information can be found on the GOV.UK web site[3].

Control of Lisdexamfetamine, Tramadol, Zaleplon, Zopiclone and Reclassification of Ketamine

On 10 June 2014, the Parliamentary Order controlling, and in the case of ketamine reclassifying the following drugs, came into force.

- lisdexamfetamine
- tramadol
- zaleplon

---

[2] http://eur-lex.europa.eu/LexUriServ/LexUriServ.do?uri=OJ:
L:2011:338:0031:0034:EN:PDF
[3] https://www.gov.uk/controls-on-torture-goods

- zopiclone
- medicines containing these substances.

The Order, available on legislation.gov.uk (external link), controls:

- lisdexamphetamine as a Class B drug
- tramadol as a Class C drug
- zopiclone and zaleplon as Class C drugs.

The Order also reclassifies ketamine as a Class B drug under the Misuse of Drugs Act 1971.

Companies who possess, supply or produce lisdexamfetamine, tramadol, zaleplon, zopiclone (or medicines containing these substances) need to get the correct licences from the Home Office.

More information on how to apply for a licence, and how much they cost are available on www.GOV.UK at https://www.gov.uk/controlled-drugs-licences-fees-and-returns or by calling the Duty Compliance Officer on 020 7035 8972.

Companies without the correct licences are at risk of prosecution.

The listed drugs will be scheduled, alongside their control, as follows to ensure that they remain available for use in healthcare:

- lisdexamfetamine (a drug which converts to dexamfetamine when administered orally and used as second line treatment for ADHD) will be listed in Schedule 2 alongside dexamfetamine
- tramadol will be listed in Schedule 3 but exempted from the safe custody requirements. Full prescription writing requirements under regulation 15 will apply to its use in healthcare,
- zopiclone and zaleplon will be listed in Part 1 of Schedule 4 alongside zolpidem.

Ketamine is not being rescheduled immediately. In line with the Advisory Council on the Misuse of Drugs' (ACMD) advice, the Home Office will carry out a public consultation later this year to assess the impact of rescheduling ketamine to Schedule 2.

A final decision on the appropriate schedule for ketamine will be made after the consultation. Until then ketamine will remain a Schedule 4 Part 1 drug.

Home Office Circular 008/2014: A change to the Misuse of Drugs Act 1971 – Control of NBOMes, Benzofurans, Lisdexamphetamine, Tramadol, Zopiclone, Zaleplon and Reclassification of Ketamine[1].

---

[1] https://www.gov.uk/government/publications/circular-0082014-changes-to-the-misuse-of-drugs-act-1971

Best Practice Temperature Monitoring

Why control and monitor temperature?

1　Manufacturers subject their products to stability studies that are used to determine appropriate storage conditions including those for temperature. These conditions are therefore specific for each product, and wholesalers should refer to manufacturers' information when deciding the storage conditions to use.

　　Medicinal products experiencing an adverse temperature may undergo physical, chemical or microbiological degradation. In the most serious of cases this may lead to conversion of the medicine to ineffective or harmful forms. The ability to detect these changes may not appear until the medicine is consumed, and it is therefore essential that appropriate temperature conditions are controlled and monitored throughout each step of the supply chain.

Control and monitoring of storage areas

2　Where medicines are stored that may be required in an emergency then contingency measures should be put in place such as linking essential equipment in a large warehouse to a source of emergency power. These emergency measures should be routinely tested, such as the confirmation of restoration of stored data and settings when emergency power supply is activated and after normal power is resumed. For these products there should be a system in place to ensure that on-call personnel are notified in the event of power failure or temperature alarms being triggered including notification outside of normal working hours.

3　The application of Mean Kinetic Temperature (MKT) to temperature monitoring of wholesale products is only appropriate where an acceptable MKT value is provided by the MA holder for a specific product, and the recording of temperature can be confirmed to be consistent and complete from the moment of leaving the manufacturer's premises. In practice the application of MKT fails where a complete chain of temperature recording cannot be allocated to a specific consignment of a product. Attempts to apply MKT have been proposed by wholesalers as an alternative to having adequate temperature control within their warehouses as well as attempting to downgrade the impact of temperature excursions. The use of MKT in the wholesale environment without robust supporting information and methodology is therefore discouraged.

SMALL REFRIGERATORS

4   Refrigerators used to store pharmaceuticals should be demonstrated to be fit for purpose. In the simplest of cases a new off-the–shelf refrigerator installed according to the manufacturer's instructions and temperature monitored with an appropriate device may be considered appropriately qualified for storing cold chain product that is shown to be unaffected by minor temperature excursions. A refrigerator used for holding more susceptible stock such as biological products will require more extensive qualification.

5   In addition to temperature mapping and monitoring there should be safeguards to preserve appropriate storage conditions. Some small refrigerators are purported to be medical or pharmaceutical refrigerators but this on its own does not automatically render them suitable for wholesale use. The refrigerator should be capable of restoring the temperature quickly after the door has been opened and without danger of overshooting to extreme cold. This could be assisted by an internal fan and good shelf design which enables an efficient air flow. There should be no internal ice box and no internal temperature dials capable of being inadvertently knocked and adjusted.

6   Storage practices for using small refrigerators should include consideration of segregation of stock with different status, e.g. incoming, quarantine, returned and outgoing stock. Sufficient space should be maintained to permit adequate air circulation and product should not be stored in contact with the walls or on the floor of the refrigerator. If the refrigerator is filled to capacity the effect on temperature distribution should be investigated. Where non-refrigerated items are introduced to the refrigerator, such as non-conditioned gel packs, the impact of introducing these items should be assessed regarding the increase in temperature they cause.

LARGE COMMERCIAL REFRIGERATORS AND WALK-IN COLD ROOMS

7   These should be of appropriate design, suitably sited and be constructed with appropriate materials. The design should ensure general principles of GDP can be maintained, such as segregation of stock. Condensate from chillers should not be collected inside the unit and there should be a capability to carry out routine maintenance and service activities as much as possible from outside the unit. The temperature should be monitored with an electronic temperature-recording device that measures load temperature in one or more locations depending on the size of the unit, and alarms should be fitted to indicate power outages and temperature excursions.

FREEZERS

8   The same general principles apply to freezers as apply to other cold chain storage units above. Walk-in freezers pose a significant operator health and safety risk, and the impact of ways of working should be reviewed with consideration of risk to causing temperature excursions.

Calibration of temperature monitoring devices

9   In order to have confidence in temperature readings monitoring devices should be calibrated to demonstrate they have appropriate accuracy and precision. Temperate storage thermometers should be capable of reading $\pm1°C$, and cold chain devices capable of reading $\pm0.5°C$. Calibration should extend across the whole of the working range, so for a temperate storage range of 15°C to 25°C the calibration range may be 10°C to 30°C to allow the thermometer to be used in assessing temperature excursions or to be used in temperature mapping exercises. Results of the calibration exercise should be presented in a report or calibration certificate approved by the calibrator and demonstrated to be appropriate for use by the wholesaler. The certificate should include the following details:

- Serial number of the calibrated instrument
- Serial numbers of test instruments
- Traceability to national or international calibration standards
- Calibration test method used
- ISO or equivalent registration details of calibration laboratory
- Date of calibration
- Calibration results
- Unique certificate number
- Approval of results by calibrator.

Where a temperature monitoring device reads temperature from a main monitoring unit plus a remote probe it should be clear from the calibration certificate which part of the device the calibration refers to. Calibration should be carried out annually, and where adjustments are made to the equipment as part of calibration an assessment of accuracy and precision should be made prior to adjustment in addition to following adjustment. On completion a suitable representative from the wholesaler should approve the calibration indicating its suitability for use.

Sales Representative Samples

Under the legislation on advertising medicines, companies may only provide free samples to persons qualified to prescribe the medicine. Samples may only be supplied in response to a signed and dated request from the prescriber and must be appropriately labelled and accompanied by a copy of the Summary of Product Characteristics (SPC). The company must have adequate procedures for control and accountability for all samples. See section 6.12 of MHRA's Blue Guide for details of the legal requirements.

MHRA is aware that in some cases sales representatives receive samples to fill prescriber requests and that the medicinal products are delivered to them by colleagues or by couriers. Either way, the storage and delivery arrangements for these medicinal products must be validated to ensure the medicinal product will be transported expeditiously under controlled Good Distribution Practice (GDP) conditions and in accordance with labelled storage requirements at all times. It is highly unlikely that samples requiring refrigeration will meet these requirements. With regards to storage it is not acceptable for samples to be stored in the representative's home (on unlicensed premises, which are not GDP compliant), lacking appropriate storage facilities, security and controls to maintain the quality of the medicines and provide an audit trail.

Likewise distribution of samples involving delivery in a representative's vehicle that has no provision for maintaining correct storage conditions is also unacceptable. Temperatures in a car boot in high summer could reach 50 degrees Celsius or go below 0 degrees Celsius in winter. The practice of providing sales representatives with samples of medicinal products which they retain for onward distribution is therefore unlikely to be acceptable due to the storage and transport difficulties outlined above. The only reason for which sales representatives may hold samples on a long-term basis is for the purpose of product identification. In this regard procedures must be in place to ensure accountability for any such stock and to ensure no packs are provided to healthcare professionals.

Handling Returns of Non-defective Medicinal Products

Any person acting as a wholesale distributor must hold a wholesale dealer's licence (WDA(H)). Article 80(g) of Directive 2001/83/EC provides that distributors of human medicines must comply with the principles of and guidelines for good distribution practice (GDP).

The Commission has revised its guidelines for GDP which are now contained in the Guidelines on Good Distribution Practice of Medicinal Products for Human Use (2013/C 343/01). Paragraph 6.3 of GDP refers to returned medicinal products, the key elements being that; "products that have left the premises of the distributor should only be returned to saleable stock if...the medicinal products are in their unopened and undamaged secondary packaging and are in good condition; have not expired and have not been recalled; it has been demonstrated by the customer that the medicinal products have been transported, stored and handled in compliance with their specific storage requirements; and they have been examined and assessed by a sufficiently trained and competent person authorised to do so;"

MHRA re-affirm that a licensed site can only be interpreted as being under full GDP control at a licensed wholesale dealer's site. This applies to all categories of medicines. Medicinal products held in unlicensed storage and distribution sites are not considered to be within the licensed wholesale distribution network.

Returns from a licensed wholesale dealer's site

MHRA will adopt a pragmatic approach to the return of non defective medicinal products for those products returned from a customer operating from a licensed wholesale dealer's site.

In such circumstances, the return should be completed as expeditiously as possible and the most expedient and appropriate method of transportation must be used.

Returns from an unlicensed site

AMBIENT

For those non defective ambient medicinal products returned from an unlicensed site, the return should be completed within five days, including transport.

REFRIGERATED

For those non defective refrigerated medicinal products returned from an unlicensed site, the return should be completed within 24 hours, including transport.

The Responsible Person or the authorised person must be able to demonstrate evidence of "full knowledge" of the storage whilst at the unlicensed site, including transportation to and from the site.

Short Term Storage of Ambient and Refrigerated Medicinal Products – Requirements for a Wholesale Dealer's Licence

The EU GDP Guidelines define wholesale distribution as;
"…all activities consisting of procuring, holding, supplying or exporting medicinal products…" The annexed Glossary of Terms defines holding as "storing medicinal products".

Medicinal products should therefore only be stored on premises that are covered by a wholesale dealer's licence.

However, there are certain cases where medicinal products are held for short periods of time during transportation and prior to onward shipment e.g. in the transportation vehicle at motorway service stations or in overnight freight depots.

In such instances it has been determined that, as a matter of policy, a site does not have to be named on a licence where ambient products are stored for less than 36 hours.

Sites holding ambient products in excess of 36 hours must be licensed

This policy applies only where ownership of the products has not been transferred to the person carrying out the storage activities.

Where ownership has been transferred, this is supply and as such the receiving site must be licensed.

It is also important to note that, where wholesaling activities other than storage are being carried out, the site should be named on the relevant licence. This includes the handling of returned goods and where decisions are made regarding suitability for resale, as well as the usual activities of picking against orders.

Sites where refrigerated products are held, even when this is for less than 36 hours, must be licensed

The exception will be where these products are transported and stored overnight in continuously refrigerated vehicles.

The provisions of Chapter 9.2 of the EU GDP Guidelines must also be observed.

Qualification of Customers and Suppliers

Before commencing wholesale dealing activities with a customer or supplier (trading partners), wholesale dealers should ensure that their proposed trading partners are entitled to trade with them. Checks should demonstrate that trading partners either hold the required manufacturing and wholesale dealer's licence where necessary or that they are entitled to receive medicines for the purpose of retail supply or for use in the course of their business.

Wholesale dealers should request those trading partners that wholesale or manufacture human medicines to supply a copy of their licence before trading commences.

Subsequent and continuing bona fides checks can be made by checking against the Register of licence holders on MHRA's website.

Qualification of suppliers

Maintaining the integrity of the supply chain is one of the most important aspects of wholesale distribution. A robust fully documented system to ensure medicines are sourced appropriately must be in place and subjected to regular review. Wholesalers must ensure their suppliers are appropriately licenced to supply medicines. The qualification of suppliers requires the following steps to be fully complaint.

- The licence of the supplier should be viewed, either a copy obtained from the company or the details can be viewed on the MHRA's website that has registers of wholesalers and manufacturers.[1] Whilst MHRA registers are updated regularly they must not be relied on as a sole means of qualifying suppliers' authority to supply.
- The EudraGMDP website has daily updates from the MHRA and contains all current live licences. The EudraGMDP website does not however contain all the information on a WDA(H) that companies need to fully qualify suppliers and must not be relied on as a sole means of qualifying suppliers' authority to supply.[2]
- For supplies from other EEA member states the same checks should be made on EudraGMDP and via licences that have been translated. The translated licences should be translated and authenticated as such by a notary.

Compliance with GDP

Wholesalers must verify that wholesale suppliers comply with the principles and guidelines of good distribution practices.

- The GDP certificate of the wholesaler should be viewed on the EudraGMDP website. The date of the certificate expiry should be noted.

---

[1] http://www.mhra.gov.uk/Howweregulate/Medicines/Licensingofmedicines/Manufacturersandwholesaledealerslicences/index.htm
[2] http://eudragmdp.ema.europa.eu/inspections/logonGeneralPublic.do

- If there is no GDP certificate available then other evidence of GDP compliance by the wholesale supplier should be obtained, such as a copy of the inspection close out letter confirming GDP compliance.

Routine re-qualification

Wholesalers must be aware of issues that could affect their suppliers' continued authority to supply. The following should be carried out:

- Regular checks at least twice a month of MHRA's list of suspended licence holders.
- Regular checks on EudraGMDP website for issued GMP and GDP statements of non-compliance.
- At least annually, a documented full re-qualification of suppliers.

Due diligence

When entering into a new contract with new suppliers, the wholesale distributor should carry out 'due diligence' checks in order to assess the suitability, competence and reliability of the other party. This could include checking the financial status of the supplier.

Falsified Medicines

A "falsified medicinal product" means any medicinal product with a false representation of:

(a) its identity, including its packaging and labelling, its name or its composition (other than any unintentional quality defect) as regards any of its ingredients including excipients and the strength of those ingredients;

(b) its source, including its manufacturer, its country of manufacturing, its country of origin or its marketing authorisation holder; or

(c) its history, including the records and documents relating to the distribution channels used.

The supply of falsified medicines is a global phenomenon and one which MHRA takes very seriously. Falsified medicines represent a threat to the legitimate UK supply chain and to patient safety. They are fraudulent and may be deliberately misrepresented with respect to identity, composition and/or source. Falsification can apply to both innovator and generic products, prescription and self-medication, as well as to traditional herbal remedies. Falsified medicines may include products with the correct ingredients but fake packaging, with the wrong ingredients, without active ingredients or with insufficient active ingredients, and may even contain harmful or poisonous substances.

The supply and distribution of medicines is tightly controlled within the European Community.

All licensed wholesalers must comply with the Community's agreed standards of good distribution practice (GDP) and there exist strict licensing and regulatory requirements in UK domestic legislation to safeguard patients against potential hazards arising from poor distribution practices: for example, purchasing suspect or falsified products, failing to establish the "bona fides" of suppliers and purchasers, inadequate record keeping, and so on.

Section 6.4 of the EU Guide to GDP is of principal importance to wholesale dealers. This states:

> "Wholesale distributors must immediately inform the competent authority and the marketing authorisation holder of any medicinal products they identify as falsified or suspect to be falsified[1]. A procedure should be in place to this effect. It should be recorded with all the original details and investigated.
>
> Any falsified medicinal products found in the supply chain should immediately be physically segregated and stored in a dedicated area away from all other medicinal products. All relevant activities in relation to such products should be documented and records retained."

Wholesale dealers in particular should maintain a high level of vigilance against the procurement or supply of potentially falsified product. Such product may be offered for sale below the established market price so rigorous checks should be made on the bona fides of the supplier and the origin of the product. It is known that some wholesalers are themselves developing good practice strategies – such as conducting rigorous physical inspections of packs when grey market purchases are made – and this is encouraged. Any suspicious activity should be reported to:

Email: casereferrals@mhra.gsi.gov.uk
Telephone: +44 (0)20 3080 6330

To report suspected counterfeit medicines or medical devices:
Email: counterfeit@mhra.gsi.gov.uk
Website: www.mhra.gov.uk
Telephone: +44 (0)20 3080 6701

---

[1] Article 80(i) of Directive 2001/83/EC.

Regulatory Action

The competent authority will take regulatory action where breaches of legislation are identified; this may take the form of adverse licensing action e.g. make a variation to an existing licence, suspension or revocation of a licence and/or the instigation of criminal proceedings.

Diverted Medicines

Diversion is the term used for the fraudulent activity where medicines destined for non-EU markets re-enter the EU and are placed back on to the European market at a higher price.

The diversion of medicines involves medicinal products being offered at preferential prices and exported to specific markets (normally third countries) outside the EU. Diversion occurs when unscrupulous traders, on receipt of the medicines, re-export the products back to the EU – with the consequence that patients for whom these preferentially-priced medicines were intended, are denied access to them. Such products appearing on the EU market are then known as "diverted" from their intended market. This represents not only a corrupt diversion for profit, but such activity also poses the risk of inappropriate or unlicensed use, and the risk that the product may also be compromised due to poor storage and transportation.

As with counterfeit products, wholesale dealers in particular should maintain a high level of vigilance against the procurement or supply of potentially diverted product. Diverted products may be offered for sale below the established market value, therefore appropriate checks should be made on the bona fides of the supplier and the origin of the product should be ascertained.

Parallel Distribution

Parallel distribution embodies two fundamental principles of the European Community's founding Treaty (of Rome): the free movement of goods and Community-wide exhaustion of intellectual property rights. It is also referred to as parallel trade and also, less correctly (since the EEA[1] is a single market with no internal borders), as parallel import or export.

Parallel distribution exists in the absence of price harmonisation of pharmaceutical products within the European Union, i.e. when there are

---

[1] The member states of the European Union plus Iceland, Norway and Liechtenstein.

significant price differences between countries; this is the case in the European Union, where prices of medicines are not governed by free competition laws, but are generally fixed by the government.

It involves the transfer of genuine, original branded products, authorised in accordance with Community legislation, marketed in one Member State of the EEA at a lower price (the source country) to another EEA member state (the country of destination) by a parallel distributor, and placed on the market in competition with a therapeutically identical product already marketed there at a higher price by or under licence from the owner of the brand.

The pharmaceutical products which are distributed in this way are identical in all respects to the branded version marketed by the originator in the country into which it is imported. They are not copies; they do not vary in any respect from the original; and they are manufactured normally by the originator or by the licensee to the approved product specification. All such products require a Product Licence for Parallel Import (PLPI) which is a "piggy-back" authorisation granted by the competent regulatory authority (MHRA in the UK), after extensive checks to ensure that the imported drug is therapeutically the same as the domestic version.

Parallel distributors operating in the UK are subject to a system of licensing and inspection, which ensures that licensed medicinal products conform to internationally agreed standards, and that those medicines are stored and distributed in compliance with the required regulatory standards. Distributors are required to hold a wholesale dealer's licence, in accordance with Article 77 of Directive 2001/83/EC, as amended. The only exception is if a manufacturing authorisation includes provision for wholesale dealing. In accordance with the wholesaling authorisation, parallel distributors are obliged to follow GDP guidelines in accordance with Article 84 of the Directive, employ a Responsible Person and are subject to periodic inspection by the competent (licensing) authority.

In addition, parallel distributors in the country of destination (the receiving country) involved in repackaging or relabelling of product must employ at least one Qualified Person (QP), who has received the relevant education and training (in accordance with Article 48 of the Directive), with responsibility to ensure that a quality system is implemented and maintained. A Manufacturing (assembly) Authorisation is also required. Regular GMP inspections are undertaken at parallel assemblers and distributors (performing relabelling/repacking activities) by the competent authority in the Member State concerned to ensure that GMP is adhered to.

Parallel distributors are required to have effective recall procedures in place. MHRA has systems in place to receive and investigate reports of packaging and labelling problems with medicines, including parallel traded products.

Relabelling/Repackaging

The goods should remain in their original packaging as long as possible. However, once the received product is approved for processing, relabelling may be undertaken in accordance with the national simplified marketing authorisation of the parallel-distributed product, under conditions of GMP, i.e. exactly the same procedures as those followed by all pharmaceutical manufacturers.

This either involves replacement of the original outer carton with a brand new one or over-stickering the original outer carton, with both providing the approved label text in the language of the country of destination. In all cases, the existing package leaflet is removed and replaced by a new one originated by the parallel distributor in accordance with the simplified marketing authorisation in the language of the country of destination. In addition to the requirements of the PLPI marketing authorisation it may be necessary, as part of any repackaging specifications, for the applicant to address any trademark concerns that might arise. This may involve technical and commercial discussions between the trademark holder and the PLPI applicant.

Both the original cartons – if these are replaced – and the original leaflets must be destroyed. No handling of the actual product (e.g. open units of tablets or capsules) within its immediate packaging (e.g. blister or foil packs) should take place during replacement of the original carton and it is important to maintain the audit trail back to the origin.

As with any other pharmaceutical manufacturer, parallel distributor operators involved in relabelling and/or repackaging should be given regular training in GMP. Batch documentation should be retained for each batch.

Maintenance of the integrity of the supply chain

Parallel distributors should only purchase medicinal products with marketing authorisations from authorised wholesalers or manufacturers in other EEA countries. The supplying wholesaler should make available before sale a copy of its wholesale authorisation and provide assurance that the supplies were obtained from the original manufacturer and/or an authorised wholesaler within the EEA.

Parallel distributors should also only sell or supply medicinal products with marketing authorisations to authorised wholesalers, registered pharmacies or other persons entitled to sell medicinal products to the general public. A copy of the authorisation should be requested if there is any doubt.

Continued Supply

Under Article 23a of Directive 2001/83/EC, as inserted by Article 1(22) of Directive 2004/27/EC, the marketing authorisation holder is required to notify the competent authority (MHRA in the UK) of the date of actual marketing of the medicinal product, taking account of the various presentations authorised, and to notify the competent authority if the product ceases to be placed on the market either temporarily or permanently. Except in exceptional circumstances, the notification must be made no less than two months before the interruption.

Any authorisation which within three years of granting is not placed on the market will cease to be valid. In respect of generic medicinal products, the three year period will start on the grant of the authorisation, or at the end of the period of market exclusivity or patent protection of the reference product, whichever is the later date. If a product is placed on the market after authorisation, but subsequently ceases to be available on the market in the UK for a period of three consecutive years, it will also cease to be valid. In these circumstances MHRA will, however, when it is aware of the imminent expiry of the three year period, notify the marketing authorisation holder in advance that their marketing authorisation will cease to be valid. In exceptional circumstances, and on public health grounds, MHRA may grant an exemption from the invalidation of the marketing authorisation after three years. Whether there are exceptional circumstances and public health grounds for an exemption will be assessed on a case by case basis. When assessing such cases, MHRA will, in particular, consider the implications for patients and public health more generally of a marketing authorisation no longer being valid.

MHRA has received requests for advice on implications for maintaining the harmonisation of an authorisation across Member States if a presentation of a product is withdrawn from the market of the Reference Member State (RMS) and remains unavailable on that market for three years. Discussions on applying the sunset clause provision in such circumstances continue at EU level. In the meantime the MHRA will address the implications of this issue on a case by case basis.

Those provisions are implemented in the UK by Part 5 of the Human Medicines Regulations 2012.

In accordance with MHRA's interpretation of the expression "placing on the market" when used elsewhere in the Directive, MHRA's view is that a product is "placed on the market" at the first transaction by which the product enters the distribution chain in the UK. The marketing authorisation holder must, therefore, notify MHRA when a product with a new marketing authorisation is first placed into the distribution chain, rather than the first date it becomes available to individual patients.

MHRA requests that you notify us of this first "placing on the market" within one calendar month. In order to ensure that a marketing authorisation continues to be valid, the marketing authorisation holder must ensure that at least one packaging presentation (e.g. bottle or blister pack) of the product, which can include own label supplies, authorised under that marketing authorisation is present on the market.

The marketing authorisation holder must report all cessations/interruptions to MHRA. However, MHRA does not need to be notified of the following:

(a) normal seasonal changes in manufacturing and/or distribution schedules (such as cold and flu remedies);
(b) short-term temporary interruptions in placing on the market that will not affect normal availability to distributors.

If you are in doubt about whether or not you need to notify an interruption in supply, you should err on the side of caution and report it to MHRA in the normal way. You must notify MHRA if any of the presentations authorised under a single marketing authorisation cease to be placed on the market either temporarily or permanently, but, as stated above, the absence of availability of one or more presentations – as long as one presentation of the product authorised under the single marketing authorisation remains on the market – will not invalidate the marketing authorisation. Problems relating to manufacturing or assembly should also be discussed with the appropriate GMP Inspector and issues of availability of medicines relating to suspected or confirmed product defects should be directly notified to, and discussed with, the Defective Medicines Reporting Centre (Tel: 020 3080 6574).

The Department of Health (DH) also has an interest in the availability of products for supply to the NHS, and together with the Association of the British Pharmaceutical Industry (ABPI) and the British Generics Manufacturers Association (BGMA), has developed best practice guidelines for notifying medicine shortages. These guidelines, together with DH/ABPI guidelines "Ensuring Best Practice in the Notification of Product Discontinuations" complement the statutory requirements under the European legislation and may be found (in PDF format) on the DH website (www.dh.gov.uk). Marketing authorisation holders should, therefore, continue to notify the Department of Health about interruptions and cessations of marketing in accordance with these guidelines.

In this context, your attention is also drawn to Article 81 of Directive 2001/83/EC as substituted by Article 1(57) of Directive 2004/27/EC, under which the marketing authorisation holder and the distributors of a medicinal product actually placed on the market shall, within the limits of their responsibilities, ensure appropriate and continued supplies of that medicinal product to pharmacies and persons authorised to supply medicinal products so that the needs of patients in the Member State in question are covered. Failure by a marketing authorisation holder to comply with this obligation is a criminal offence, unless the marketing authorisation holder took all reasonable precautions and exercised all due diligence to avoid such a failure.

Reporting Adverse Reactions

An adverse reaction means a response to a medicinal product which is noxious and unintended. A serious adverse reaction is one which results in a person's death, threatens a person's life, results in hospitalisation, persistent or significant disability/incapacity, or results in a congenital abnormality or birth defect.

Wholesalers supplying special medicinal products (unlicensed products) are under an obligation to keep records of any adverse reaction of which they become aware and report any serious adverse reaction to the MHRA, this should be done by submission of a "Yellow Card"[1] report.

Where the product is an exempt advanced therapy medicinal product, the wholesaler is obliged to inform the MHRA of any adverse reaction of which they become aware. All records should be retained for the minimum periods required by UK legislation.

Marketing authorisation, homoeopathic registration and traditional herbal medicinal product licence holders have separate obligations in relation to tracking and reporting adverse reactions.

Product Recall/Withdrawal

Manufacturers, importers and distributors are obliged to inform the MHRA of any suspected quality defect in a medicinal product that could or would result in a recall, or restriction on supply.

A defective medicinal product is one whose quality does not conform to the requirements of its marketing authorisation, specification or for some other reason of quality is potentially hazardous. A defective product may be suspected because of a visible defect or contamination or as a result of tests performed on it, or because it has caused untoward reactions in a patient or for other reasons involving poor manufacturing or distribution practice. Falsified medicines are considered as defective products.

The Human Medicines Regulations 2012 [SI 2012/1916] imposes certain obligations on licence holders with regard to withdrawal and recall from sale. The aim of the Defective Medicines Report Centre (DMRC)

[1] http://www.mhra.gov.uk/Safetyinformation/Reportingsafetyproblems/Reportingsuspectedadversedrugreactions/index.htm

within MHRA is to minimise the hazard to patients arising from the distribution of defective (human) medicinal products by providing an emergency assessment and communications system between the suppliers (manufacturers and distributors), the regulatory authorities and the end user. The DMRC achieves this by receiving reports of suspected defective (human) medicinal products; monitoring and, as far as is necessary, directing and advising actions by the relevant licence holder(s) and communicating the details of this action with the appropriate urgency and distribution to users of the products. The communication normally used is a "Drug Alert".

Immediately a hazard is identified from any source, it will be necessary to evaluate the level of danger, and the category of recall, if required. Where the reported defect is a confirmed defect, the DMRC will then take one of the following courses of action and obtain a report from the manufacturer on the nature of the defect, their handling of the defect and action to be taken to prevent its recurrence.

Issue a "Recall"

Under normal circumstances a recall is always required where a defect is confirmed unless the defect is shown to be of a trivial nature and/or there are unlikely to be significant amounts of the affected product remaining in the market.

It is the licence holder's responsibility to recall products from customers, in a manner agreed with the DMRC. The company should provide copies of draft recall letters for agreement with the DMRC. If the company (licence holder) does not agree to a recall voluntarily, MHRA, as licensing authority, may be obliged to take compulsory action.

Issue a "Drug Alert"

Recall and withdrawal of product from the market is normally the responsibility of the licence holder. However, where a product has been distributed widely and/or there is a serious risk to health from the defect, MHRA can opt to issue a Drug Alert letter. The Drug Alert cascade mechanism ensures rapid communication of safety information; it is not a substitute for, but complementary to, any action taken by the licence holder. The text of the Alert should be agreed between MHRA and the company concerned.

In some cases, where a product has been supplied to a small number of known customers, MHRA may decide that notification will be adequate and a Drug Alert is not needed.

The DMRC may also request companies to insert notification in the professional press in certain cases.

Management of the recall

The company should directly contact wholesalers, hospitals, retail pharmacies and overseas distributors supplied. The DMRC is likely to take the lead in notifying Regional Contacts for NHS Trusts and Provider Units and Health Authorities, special and Government hospitals and overseas regulatory authorities.

The DMRC will liaise with the company and discuss arrangements for the recall, requesting the dates that supply started and ceased and a copy of any letters sent out by that company concerning the recall. Again, it is desirable that the text of the notices sent via the company and by the DMRC should be mutually agreed.

Management of Recall Activity by Wholesalers

MHRA expects key personnel, such as the Responsible Person, to keep themselves up to date with drug safety issues. This can be done for example by checking the relevant sections of MHRA's web site daily or alternatively by signing up for relevant MHRA email alerts.

Wholesalers and brokers should retain records of all recall notices received and/or reviewed, including those notices for which no action is required.

Recall processes should be designed with quality management in mind, for example change control and risk management should be applied for significant changes such as a change of Responsible Person or nominated deputy, changes to product handling/storage, or changes to transport arrangements. At such times there should be an assessment of whether a test recall should be performed to provide assurance of the ongoing effectiveness of the company's processes and identify any weaknesses or areas for improvement.

Chapter 6 section 5 of the EU GDP Guidelines[1] describes the minimum standards for wholesalers in relation to recall activities.

When the wholesaler receives a drug alert or recall notice they should take steps to:

- follow the detail of the recall message;
- identify any affected stock on site or in transit (including that returned from customers);
- identify any customers to whom the affected products have been supplied, including where products may have been supplied as samples;

---

[1] Guidelines of 5 November 2013 on Good Distribution Practice of medicinal products for human use (2013/C 343/01)

- directly contact those customers, making them aware of the details of the recall and where necessary providing a mechanism for returning affected stock;
- physically segregate and quarantine any affected product in an area away from other medicinal products, ensuring that such stock does not re-enter the supply chain;
- reconcile the quantities of stock purchased, onsite, sent out and returned;
- keep recall notices open for an appropriate period, so as to capture any affected stock still moving through the supply chain.

All recall activities should be documented at the time they occur and at the conclusion of all recall activities the Responsible Person (or their nominated deputy) should produce a report, making an objective assessment of whether the recall process achieved its objectives and identifying any areas requiring improvement.

Management of Recall Activity by Brokers

Chapter 10 of the EU GDP Guidelines deals with brokers, and includes the requirement for the broker to have in place "...an emergency plan which ensures effective recall of medicinal products from the market...". The guidelines go on to specify that brokers should have a written procedure for supporting recalls, alongside an obligation to maintain relevant documentation.

As brokers do not hold or handle stock the scope of their recall activities are somewhat more limited than wholesalers.

A broker should:

- follow the detail of the recall message;
- identify those persons or companies involved in relevant brokered deals;
- directly contact those customers, making them aware of the details of the recall;
- keep recall notices open for an appropriate period, so as to capture any affected stock still moving through the supply chain.

As with wholesalers all recall activities should be documented at the time they occur and at the conclusion of all recall activities the Broker should produce a report, making an objective assessment of whether the recall process achieved its objectives and identifying any areas requiring improvement.

Supply and brokering to countries outside of the UK

Where wholesale stock has been supplied or brokered to countries outside of the UK, there are the same obligations to contact the relevant customers to make them aware of the recall. It should be noted that certainly within the EEA, dependent on the nature of the recall and its impact on product availability and patient health, different countries may take varying levels of action. The wholesaler or broker should confirm with the relevant competent authority the particular terms of a recall in a particular territory.

Testing the recall process

Section 6.5 of the EU GDP Guidelines requires that "the effectiveness of the arrangements for product recall should be evaluated regularly (at least annually)".

The aim of such an evaluation should be to challenge the internal processes of the licence holder as far as practicable. This is particularly important in organisations where recall activities occur infrequently, for example where the product range handled is limited in quantity or scope. Where stock is held on behalf of a licence holder at a third party site then the recall test should extend to covering activities at the third party site, this will require a degree of liaison between both sites' Responsible Persons.

The test process should be described in the company's quality system in sufficient detail to allow staff to perform the test and to be able to assess the progress of the recall process at each step.

It is expected that as a minimum the test process should mimic a real recall but should stop short of contacting the licence holder's customers. The product and batch selected should be typical of those handled by the company in the previous 12 months and where possible provide a worst case scenario (for example when key staff are absent or for essential medicines when alternative supplies may need to be made available). Correspondence (for example emails to staff at a branch level) should, as far as practicable, not indicate that it is being used for test purposes.

The test process should be documented so as to be able to demonstrate that:

- staff can receive information effectively and act on it quickly;
- stock in question can be identified, reconciled and segregated effectively;
- customers supplied with the stock can be identified quickly from records, and their most up-to-date contact details confirmed (including address and telephone details both inside and outside working hours);
- adherence to the company's recall process has taken place;
- the effectiveness of training can be assessed.

For the purposes of a test recall the MHRA does not normally expect licence holders to contact their customers as this could lead to unintended consequences should the customer believe the test recall to be real. Instead, the licence holder should obtain evidence that the contact details (physical address, telephone/fax numbers, email address) they hold for the relevant customers are up-to-date. Where the licence holder would send a letter/fax/email to their customer with the details of the recall, this should be drafted but not sent.

Where customers are contacted, there should be adequate oversight of the entire test process to ensure that misunderstandings do not occur.

As with all routine recall activities, at the conclusion of test recall activities the Responsible Person should produce a report, making an objective assessment of whether the recall process achieved its objectives and identifying any areas requiring improvement.

It may be possible for a company to use recall activities for non-medicinal products to demonstrate an effective recall process, providing that the process described in the company's quality system covers the handling of both medicinal and non-medicinal products in the same manner and leads to the same outcome.

Follow-up action

The DMRC will monitor the conduct and success of the recall by the manufacturer or distributor. As follow-up action, it may be necessary to consider any or all of the following:

- arrange a visit to the licence holder/manufacturer/distributor;
- arrange a visit to the point of discovery of the defect;
- refer to the Inspectorate to arrange an inspection;
- seek special surveillance of adverse reaction reports;
- refer the matter for adverse licensing and/or enforcement action.

Reporting a suspected defect

Suspected defects can be reported by telephone, e-mail or letter or using our online form:

Address:
DMRC, 151 Buckingham Palace Road, London, SW1W 9SZ, UK.
Telephone: +44 (0)20 3080 6574 (08:45 – 16:45 Monday to Friday)
Telephone: +44 (0)7795 641532 (urgent calls outside working hours, at weekends or on public holidays)
E-mail: dmrc@mhra.gsi.gov.uk
Online form: www.mhra.gov.uk
http://www.mhra.gov.uk/Safetyinformation/Reportingsafetyproblems/Reportingsuspecteddefectsinmedicines/Suspecteddefectonlineform/index.htm

UK Guidance on Brokering Medicines

Contents

Introduction

Persons procuring, holding, storing, supplying or exporting medicinal products are required to hold a wholesale distribution authorisation in accordance with Directive 2001/83/EC which lays down the rules for the wholesale distribution of medicinal products in the Union.

However, the distribution network for medicinal products may involve operators who are not necessarily authorised wholesale distributors. To ensure the reliability of the supply chain, Directive 2011/62/EU, the Falsified Medicines Directive extends medicine legislation to the entire supply chain. This now includes not only wholesale distributors, whether or not they physically handle the medicinal products, but also brokers who are involved in the sale or purchase of medicinal products without selling or purchasing those products themselves, and without owning and physically handling the medicinal products.

Brokering in Medicinal Products

Brokering of medicinal products is defined in the Falsified Medicines Directive and means:

All activities in relation to the sale or purchase of medicinal products, except for wholesale distribution, that do not include physical handling and that consist of negotiating independently and on behalf of another legal or natural person.

To accord with the Directive brokers may only broker medicinal products that are the subject of an authorisation granted by the European Commission or a National Competent Authority.

Brokers should be established at a permanent address and have contact details in the EU and may only operate following registration of these details with the National Competent Authority. In the UK this is MHRA. A broker must provide required details for registration which will include their name, corporate name and permanent address. They must also notify any changes without unnecessary delay. This is to ensure the brokers accurate identification, location, communication and supervision of their activities by the National Competent Authorities.

Brokers can negotiate between the manufacturer and a wholesaler, or one wholesaler and another wholesaler, or the manufacturer or wholesale dealer with a person who may lawfully sell those products by retail or may lawfully supply them in circumstances corresponding to retail sale or a person who may lawfully administer those products.

Brokers are not virtual wholesale dealers; the definition of "Brokering medicinal products" specifically excludes the activity of "wholesale dealing". Wholesale dealing and brokering of medicinal products are separate activities. Therefore wholesale dealers who wish to broker will require a separate registration, because:

- EU legislation defines wholesale distribution and brokering a medicinal product separately;
- wholesale dealers are licensed;
- the brokering of medicinal products is subject to registration.

Registration

UK based companies that broker medicinal products and are involved in the sale or purchase of medicinal products without selling or purchasing those products themselves, and without owning and physically handling the medicinal products are considered to be brokers and will have to register with MHRA.

In order to register in the UK, brokers will have a permanent address and contact details in the UK and will only be allowed to operate as a bona fide broker following their successful registration with MHRA.

Application for Brokering Registration

The registration regime for UK brokers is subject to an application procedure, followed by a determination procedure completed by MHRA. The application procedure will include:

- making an application for registration;
- assessment by MHRA of the application;

- providing specific evidence to check bona fides;
- advising an applicant of the decision.

UK brokers may be subject to inspection at their registered premises. This will be under a risk-based inspection programme. Once registered a broker's registration will be recognised by other Member States and will allow the broker to broker across the EEA. UK medicines legislation in respect of brokering will also recognise registered brokers in other EEA Member States in the same way.

MHRA has an obligation to enter the information on a publicly accessible UK register following the determination of successful application for registration.

This publicly available UK register is required to enable National Competent Authorities in other EEA Member States to establish the bona fides and compliance of brokers established in the UK where they are involved in the sale or purchase of medicines on their territories and the UK will investigate complaints of non-compliance. Reciprocal arrangements will apply for brokers established in other Member States involved in the sale or purchase of medicines to and from the UK.

Criteria of Broker's Registration

A person may not broker a medicinal product unless that product is covered by an authorisation granted under Regulation (EC) No 726/2004 or by a competent authority of an EEA Member State and that person is validly registered as a broker with a competent authority of an EEA Member State.

A broker is not validly registered if the broker's permanent address is not entered into a register of brokers kept by a competent authority of a member State or the registration is suspended or the broker has notified the competent authority of an EEA Member State to remove them from the register.

Brokers must satisfy all the conditions of brokering and:

- have a permanent address in the UK;
- have an emergency plan which ensures effective implementation of any recall from the market ordered by the competent authorities or carried out in cooperation with the manufacturer or marketing authorisation holder for the medicinal product concerned;
- keep records either in the form of purchase/sales invoices or on computer, or in any other form, giving for any transaction in medicinal products brokered at least the following information:
  - date on which the sale or purchase of the product is brokered;
  - name of the medicinal product;

- quantity brokered;
- name and address of the supplier or consignee, as appropriate;
- batch number of the medicinal products at least for products bearing the safety features referred to in point (o) of Article 54 of Directive 2001/83/EC;
- keep the records available to the competent authorities, for inspection purposes, for a period of five years;
- comply with the principles and guidelines of good distribution practice for medicinal products as laid down in Article 84 of Directive 2001/83/EC;
- maintain a quality system setting out responsibilities, processes and risk management measures in relation to their activities.

Where the address at which the plan or records necessary to comply with the provisions of brokering are kept is different from the address notified in accordance with the application, the broker must ensure that the plan or records are kept at an address in the UK and inform the licensing authority of the address at which the plan or records are kept.

The broker must provide such information as may be requested by MHRA concerning the type and quantity of medicinal products brokered within the period specified by MHRA.

The broker must take all reasonable precautions and exercise all due diligence to ensure that any information provided by that broker to MHRA is not false or misleading.

For the purposes of enabling MHRA to determine whether there are grounds for suspending, revoking or varying the registration, the broker must permit a person authorised in writing by MHRA, on production of identification, to carry out any inspection, or to take any copies, which an inspector may carry out or take under the provisions of the Human Medicines Regulations 2012 [SI 2012/1916].

Provision of Information

Once registered, a broker will have to notify MHRA of any changes to the details for registration which might affect compliance with the requirements of the legislation in respect of brokering without unnecessary delay. This notification will be subject to a variation procedure. Responsibility for notifying MHRA of any changes lies with the person responsible for management of the brokering activities.

The person responsible for management of the brokering activities shall be required to submit a report which shall include:

- a declaration that the broker has in place appropriate systems to ensure compliance with the requirements for brokering;

- provide the details of the systems which it has in place to ensure such compliance.

An annual compliance report will need to be submitted in relation to any application made before 31st March 2014, the date of the application and in relation to each subsequent reporting year, by the 30th April following the end of that year. The annual compliance report will be subject to a variation procedure so that the broker can change the original details provided.

The broker must without delay notify the licensing authority of any changes to the matters in respect of which evidence has been supplied in relation to the compliance report which might affect compliance with the requirements of brokering.

The broker must immediately inform MHRA and the marketing authorisation holder, of medicinal products they are offered which they identify as falsified or suspect to be falsified.

Good Distribution Practice

The Commission's guidelines on good distribution practice, referred to in Article 84 of Directive 2001/83/EC have been updated to include specific provisions for brokering, see Chapter 5.

Legislation on Wholesale Distribution and Brokering Medicines

CHAPTER

8

EU Legislation on Wholesale Distribution and Brokering Medicines

Contents

DIRECTIVE 2001/83/EC, AS AMENDED, TITLE VII, WHOLESALE DISTRIBUTION AND BROKERING MEDICINES

Directive 2001/83/EC of the European Parliament and of the Council of 6 November 2001 on the Community code relating to medicinal products for human use as amended

Title VII: Wholesale Distribution and Brokering of Medicinal Products

Editor's note   Title VII of this Directive is reproduced below. Title VII has been amended by Directive 2011/62/EU and Directive 2012/26/EU. A new article 85a extends the need for a Wholesale Dealer's Licence for the export of medicine to a non-EEA country and to "introduced" medicines that are imported from a non-EEA country for the purpose of export back to a non-EEA country. A new article 85b introduces measures for persons brokering medicinal products. Reference should be made to the full Directive 2001/83/EC as amended for the preamble, definitions and the general and final provisions.

Article 76

1   Without prejudice to Article 6, Member States shall take all appropriate action to ensure that only medicinal products in respect of which a marketing authorization has been granted in accordance with Community law are distributed on their territory.

2   In the case of wholesale distribution and storage, medicinal products shall be covered by a marketing authorisation granted pursuant to Regulation (EC) No. 726/2004 or by the competent authorities of a Member State in accordance with this Directive.

3   Any distributor, not being the marketing authorisation holder, who imports a medicinal product from another Member State shall notify the marketing authorisation holder and the competent authority in the Member State to which the medicinal product will be imported of his intention to import that product. In the case of medicinal products which have not been granted an authorisation pursuant to Regulation (EC) No 726/2004, the notification to the competent authority shall be without prejudice to additional procedures provided for in the legislation of that Member State and to fees payable to the competent authority for examining the notification.

4   In the case of medicinal products which have been granted an authorisation pursuant to Regulation (EC) No 726/2004, the distributor shall submit the notification in accordance with paragraph 3 of this Article to the marketing authorisation holder and the Agency. A fee shall be payable to the Agency for checking that the conditions laid down in Union legislation on medicinal products and in the marketing authorisations are observed.

Article 77

1 Member States shall take all appropriate measures to ensure that the wholesale distribution of medicinal products is subject to the possession of an authorisation to engage in activity as a wholesaler in medicinal products, stating the premises located on their territory for which it is valid.

2 Where persons authorized or entitled to supply medicinal products to the public may also, under national law, engage in wholesale business, such persons shall be subject to the authorization provided for in paragraph 1.

3 Possession of a manufacturing authorization shall include authorization to distribute by wholesale the medicinal products covered by that authorization. Possession of an authorization to engage in activity as a wholesaler in medicinal products shall not give dispensation from the obligation to possess a manufacturing authorization and to comply with the conditions set out in that respect, even where the manufacturing or import business is secondary.

4 Member States shall enter the information relating to the authorisations referred to in paragraph 1 of this Article in the Union database referred to in Article 111(6). At the request of the Commission or any Member State, Member States shall provide all appropriate information concerning the individual authorisations which they have granted under paragraph 1 of this Article.

5 Checks on the persons authorised to engage in activity as a wholesaler in medicinal products, and the inspection of their premises, shall be carried out under the responsibility of the Member State which granted the authorisation for premises located on its territory.

6 The Member State which granted the authorization referred to in paragraph 1 shall suspend or revoke that authorization if the conditions of authorization cease to be met. It shall forthwith inform the other Member States and the Commission thereof.

7 Should a Member State consider that, in respect of a person holding an authorization granted by another Member State under the terms of paragraph 1, the conditions of authorization are not, or are no longer met, it shall forthwith inform the Commission and the other Member State involved. The latter shall take the measures necessary and shall inform the Commission and the first Member State of the decisions taken and the reasons for those decisions.

Article 78

Member States shall ensure that the time taken for the procedure for examining the application for the distribution authorization does not exceed 90 days from the day on which the competent authority of the Member State concerned receives the application.

The competent authority may, if need be, require the applicant to supply all necessary information concerning the conditions of authorization. Where the authority exercises this option, the period laid down in the first paragraph shall be suspended until the requisite additional data have been supplied.

Article 79

In order to obtain the distribution authorization, applicants must fulfil the following minimum requirements:

(a) they must have suitable and adequate premises, installations and equipment, so as to ensure proper conservation and distribution of the medicinal products;

(b) they must have staff, and in particular, a qualified person designated as responsible, meeting the conditions provided for by the legislation of the Member State concerned;

(c) they must undertake to fulfil the obligations incumbent on them under the terms of Article 80.

Article 80

Holders of the distribution authorization must fulfil the following minimum requirements:

(a) they must make the premises, installations and equipment referred to in Article 79(a) accessible at all times to the persons responsible for inspecting them;

(b) they must obtain their supplies of medicinal products only from persons who are themselves in possession of the distribution authorization or who are exempt from obtaining such authorization under the terms of Article 77(3);

(c) they must supply medicinal products only to persons who are themselves in possession of the distribution authorization or who are authorized or entitled to supply medicinal products to the public in the Member State concerned;

(ca) they must verify that the medicinal products received are not falsified by checking the safety features on the outer packaging, in accordance with the requirements laid down in the delegated acts referred to in Article 54a(2);

(d) they must have an emergency plan which ensures effective implementation of any recall from the market ordered by the competent authorities or carried out in cooperation with the manufacturer or marketing authorization holder for the medicinal product concerned;

(e) they must keep records either in the form of purchase/sales invoices or on computer, or in any other form, giving for any transaction in medicinal products received, dispatched or brokered at least the following information:

- date,
- name of the medicinal product,
- quantity received, supplied or brokered,
- name and address of the supplier or consignee, as appropriate,
- batch number of the medicinal products at least for products bearing the safety features referred to in point (o) of Article 54;

(f) they must keep the records referred to under (e) available to the competent authorities, for inspection purposes, for a period of five years;

(g) they must comply with the principles and guidelines of good distribution practice for medicinal products as laid down in Article 84.

(h) they must maintain a quality system setting out responsibilities, processes and risk management measures in relation to their activities;

(i) they must immediately inform the competent authority and, where applicable, the marketing authorisation holder, of medicinal products they receive or are offered which they identify as falsified or suspect to be falsified.

For the purposes of point (b), where the medicinal product is obtained from another wholesale distributor, wholesale distribution authorisation holders must verify compliance with the principles and guidelines of good distribution practices by the supplying wholesale distributor. This includes verifying whether the supplying wholesale distributor holds a wholesale distribution authorisation.

Where the medicinal product is obtained from the manufacturer or importer, wholesale distribution authorisation holders must verify that the manufacturer or importer holds a manufacturing authorisation.

Where the medicinal product is obtained through brokering, the wholesale distribution authorisation holders must verify that the broker involved fulfils the requirements set out in this Directive.

Article 81

With regard to the supply of medicinal products to pharmacists and persons authorised or entitled to supply medicinal products to the public, Member States shall not impose upon the holder of a distribution authorisation which has been granted by another Member State any obligation, in particular public service obligations, more stringent than those they impose on persons whom they have themselves authorised to engage in equivalent activities.

The holder of a marketing authorisation for a medicinal product and the distributors of the said medicinal product actually placed on the market in a Member State shall, within the limits of their responsibilities, ensure appropriate and continued supplies of that medicinal product to pharmacies and persons authorised to supply medicinal products so that the needs of patients in the Member State in question are covered.

The arrangements for implementing this Article should, moreover, be justified on grounds of public health protection and be proportionate in relation to the objective of such protection, in compliance with the Treaty rules, particularly those concerning the free movement of goods and competition.

Article 82

For all supplies of medicinal products to a person authorized or entitled to supply medicinal products to the public in the Member State concerned, the authorized wholesaler must enclose a document that makes it possible to ascertain:

- batch number of the medicinal products at least for products bearing the safety features referred to in point (o) of Article 54;
- the date;
- the name and pharmaceutical form of the medicinal product;
- the quantity supplied;
- the name and address of the supplier and consignor.

Member States shall take all appropriate measures to ensure that persons authorized or entitled to supply medicinal products to the public are able to provide information that makes it possible to trace the distribution path of every medicinal product.

Article 83

The provisions of this Title shall not prevent the application of more stringent requirements laid down by Member States in respect of the wholesale distribution of:

- narcotic or psychotropic substances within their territory;
- medicinal products derived from blood;
- immunological medicinal products;
- radiopharmaceuticals.

Article 84

The Commission shall publish guidelines on good distribution practice. To this end, it shall consult the Committee for Medicinal Products for Human Use and the Pharmaceutical Committee established by Council Decision 75/320/EEC.[1]

Article 85

This Title shall apply to homeopathic medicinal products.

Article 85a

In the case of wholesale distribution of medicinal products to third countries, Article 76 and point (c) of the first paragraph of Article 80 shall not apply. Moreover, points (b) and (ca) of the first paragraph of Article 80 shall not apply where a product is directly received from a third country but not imported. However, in that case wholesale distributors shall ensure that the medicinal products are obtained only from persons who are authorised or entitled to supply medicinal products in accordance with the applicable legal and administrative provisions of the third country concerned. Where wholesale distributors supply medicinal products to persons in third countries, they shall ensure that such supplies are only made to persons who are authorised or entitled to receive medicinal products for wholesale distribution or supply to the public in accordance with the applicable legal and administrative provisions of the third country concerned. The requirements set out in Article 82 shall apply to the supply of medicinal products to persons in third countries authorised or entitled to supply medicinal products to the public.

---

[1] OJ L 147, 9.6.1975, p. 23.

Article 85b

1   Persons brokering medicinal products shall ensure that the brokered medicinal products are covered by a marketing authorisation granted pursuant to Regulation (EC) No 726/2004 or by the competent authorities of a Member State in accordance with this Directive.

Persons brokering medicinal products shall have a permanent address and contact details in the Union, so as to ensure accurate identification, location, communication and supervision of their activities by competent authorities.

The requirements set out in points (d) to (i) of Article 80 shall apply *mutatis mutandis* to the brokering of medicinal products.

2   Persons may only broker medicinal products if they are registered with the competent authority of the Member State of their permanent address referred to in paragraph 1. Those persons shall submit, at least, their name, corporate name and permanent address in order to register. They shall notify the competent authority of any changes thereof without unnecessary delay.

Persons brokering medicinal products who had commenced their activity before 2 January 2013 shall register with the competent authority by 2 March 2013.

The competent authority shall enter the information referred to in the first subparagraph in a register that shall be publicly accessible.

3   The guidelines referred to in Article 84 shall include specific provisions for brokering.

4   This Article shall be without prejudice to Article 111. Inspections referred to in Article 111 shall be carried out under the responsibility of the Member State where the person brokering medicinal products is registered.

If a person brokering medicinal products does not comply with the requirements set out in this Article, the competent authority may decide to remove that person from the register referred to in paragraph 2. The competent authority shall notify that person thereof.

UK Legislation on Wholesale Distribution

Contents

The Human Medicines Regulations 2012 [SI 2012/1916]

Editor's note   These extracts from the Regulations and Standard Provisions of the Human Medicines Regulations 2012 [SI 2012/1916] are presented for the reader's convenience. Reproduction is with the permission of HMSO and the Queen's Printer for Scotland. For any definitive information reference must be made to the original Regulations. The numbering and content within this section corresponds with the regulations set out in the published Statutory Instrument (SI 2012 No.1916).

Citation and commencement

1 (1) These Regulations may be cited as the Human Medicines Regulations 2012.

(2) These Regulations come into force on 14th August 2012.

General interpretation

8   (1)   In these Regulations (unless the context otherwise requires):

"the 2001 Directive" means Directive 2001/83/EC of the European Parliament and of the Council on the Community Code relating to medicinal products for human use;

"Article 126a authorisation" means an authorisation granted by the licensing authority under Part 8 of these Regulations;

"brokering" means all activities in relation to the sale or purchase of medicinal products, except for wholesale distribution, that do not include physical handling and that consist of negotiating independently and on behalf of another legal or natural person;

"Directive 2002/98/EC" means Directive 2002/98/EC of the European Parliament and of the Council of 27 January 2003 setting standards of quality and safety for the collection, testing, processing, storage and distribution of human blood and blood components and amending Directive 2001/83/EC;

"Directive 2004/23/EC" means Directive 2004/23/EC of the European Parliament and of the Council of 31 March 2004 on setting standards of quality and safety for the donation, procurement, testing, processing, preservation, storage and distribution of human tissues and cells;

"electronic communication" means a communication transmitted (whether from one person to another, from one device to another or from a person to a device or vice versa):

(a) by means of an electronic communications network within the meaning of section 32(1) of the Communications Act 2003; or

(b) by other means but while in an electronic form;

"EU marketing authorisation" means a marketing authorisation granted or renewed by the European Commission under Regulation (EC) No 726/2004;

"European Economic Area" or "EEA" means the European Economic Area created by the EEA agreement;

"exempt advanced therapy medicinal product" has the meaning given in regulation 171;

"export" means export, or attempt to export, from the United Kingdom, whether by land, sea or air;

"falsified medicinal product" means any medicinal product with a false representation of:

(a) its identity, including its packaging and labelling, its name or its composition (other than any unintentional quality defect) as regards any of its ingredients including excipients and the strength of those ingredients;

(b) its source, including its manufacturer, its country of manufacturing, its country of origin or its marketing authorisation holder; or

(c) its history, including the records and documents relating to the distribution channels used;

"Fees Regulations" means the Medicines (Products for Human Use) (Fees) Regulations 2013[1];

"herbal medicinal product" means a medicinal product whose only active ingredients are herbal substances or herbal preparations (or both);

"herbal preparation" means a preparation obtained by subjecting herbal substances to processes such as extraction, distillation, expression, fractionation, purification, concentration or fermentation, and includes a comminuted or powdered herbal substance, a tincture, an extract, an essential oil, an expressed juice or a processed exudate;

"herbal substance" means a plant or part of a plant, algae, fungi or lichen, or an unprocessed exudate of a plant, defined by the plant part used and the botanical name of the plant, either fresh or dried, but otherwise unprocessed;

"homoeopathic medicinal product" means a medicinal product prepared from homoeopathic stocks in accordance with a homoeopathic manufacturing procedure described by:

(a) the European Pharmacopoeia; or

(b) in the absence of such a description in the European Pharmacopoeia, in any pharmacopoeia used officially in an EEA State;

"import" means import, or attempt to import, into the UK, whether by land, sea or air;

"inspector" means a person authorised in writing by an enforcement authority for the purposes of Part 16 (enforcement) (and references to "the enforcement authority", in relation to an inspector, are to the enforcement authority by whom the inspector is so authorised);

"the licensing authority" has the meaning given by regulation 6(2);

"manufacturer's licence" has the meaning given by regulation 17(1);

"marketing authorisation" means:

(a) a UK marketing authorisation; or

(b) an EU marketing authorisation;

"medicinal product subject to general sale" has the meaning given in regulation 5(1) (classification of medicinal products);

[1] S.I. 2013/532.

"Regulation (EC) No 726/2004" means Regulation (EC) No 726/2004 of the European Parliament and of the Council of 31 March 2004 laying down Community procedures for the authorisation and supervision of medicinal products for human and veterinary use and establishing a European Medicines Agency;

"Regulation (EC) No 1394/2007" means Regulation (EC) No 1394/2007 of the European Parliament and of the Council of 13 November 2007 on advanced therapy medicinal products and amending Directive 2001/83/EC and Regulation (EC) No 726/2004

"Regulation (EC) No 1234/2008" means Commission Regulation (EC) No 1234/2008 of 24 November 2008 concerning the examination of variations to the terms of marketing authorisations for medicinal products for human use and veterinary medicinal products;

"the relevant EU provisions" means the provisions of legislation of the European Union relating to medicinal products for human use except to the extent that any other enactment provides for any function in relation to any such provision to be exercised otherwise than by the licensing authority;

"relevant European State" means an EEA State or Switzerland;

"relevant medicinal product" has the meaning given by regulation 48

"special medicinal product" means a product within the meaning of regulation 167 or any equivalent legislation in an EEA State other than the UK;

"third country" means a country or territory outside the EEA:

"traditional herbal medicinal product" means a herbal medicinal product to which regulation 125 applies;

"traditional herbal registration" means a traditional herbal registration granted by the licensing authority under these Regulations;

"UK marketing authorisation" means a marketing authorisation granted by the licensing authority under:

(a) Part 5 of these Regulations; or

(b) Chapter 4 of Title III to the 2001 Directive (mutual recognition and decentralised procedure);

"wholesale dealer's licence" has the meaning given by regulation 18(1)

(2) In these Regulations, references to distribution of a product by way of wholesale dealing are to be construed in accordance with regulation 18(7) and (8).

(3) In these Regulations, references to selling by retail, or to retail sale, are references to selling a product to a person who buys it otherwise than for a purpose specified in regulation 18(8).

(4) In these Regulations, references to supplying anything in circumstances corresponding to retail sale are references to supplying it

otherwise than by way of sale, to a person who receives it otherwise than for a purpose specified in regulation 18(8);

Conditions for wholesale dealer's licence

42   (1)   Regulations 43 to 45 apply to the holder of a wholesale dealer's licence (referred to in those regulations as "the licence holder") and have effect as if they were provisions of the licence (but the provisions specified in paragraph (2) do not apply to the holder of a wholesale dealer's licence insofar as the licence relates to exempt advanced therapy medicinal products).

     (2)   Those provisions are regulations 43(2) and (8) and 44.

     (3)   The requirements in Part 2 of Schedule 6 apply to the holder of a wholesale dealer's licence insofar as the licence relates to exempt advanced therapy medicinal products, and have effect as if they were provisions of the licence.

Obligations of licence holder

43   (1)   The licence holder must comply with the guidelines on good distribution practice published by the European Commission in accordance with Article 84 of the 2001 Directive.

     (2)   The licence holder must ensure, within the limits of the holder's responsibility, the continued supply of medicinal products to pharmacies, and other persons who may lawfully sell medicinal products by retail or supply them in circumstances corresponding to retail sale, so that the needs of patients in the United Kingdom are met.

     (3)   The licence holder must provide and maintain such staff, premises, equipment and facilities for the handling, storage and distribution of medicinal products under the licence as are necessary:
       (a) to maintain the quality of the products; and
       (b) to ensure their proper distribution.

     (4)   The licence holder must inform the licensing authority of any proposed structural alteration to, or discontinuance of use of, premises to which the licence relates or which have otherwise been approved by the licensing authority.

     (5)   Subject to paragraph (6), the licence holder must not sell or supply a medicinal product, or offer it for sale or supply, unless:
       (a) there is a marketing authorisation, Article 126a authorisation, certificate of registration or traditional herbal registration (an "authorisation") in force in relation to the product; and

(b) the sale or supply, or offer for sale or supply, is in accordance with the authorisation.

(6) The restriction in paragraph (5) does not apply to:

(a) the sale or supply, or offer for sale or supply, of a special medicinal product;

(b) the export to an EEA State, or supply for the purposes of such export, of a medicinal product which may be placed on the market in that State without a marketing authorisation, Article 126a authorisation, certificate of registration or traditional herbal registration by virtue of legislation adopted by that State under Article 5(1) of the 2001 Directive; or

(c) the sale or supply, or offer for sale or supply, of an unauthorised medicinal product where the Secretary of State has temporarily authorised the distribution of the product under regulation 174.

(7) The licence holder must:

(a) keep documents relating to the sale or supply of medicinal products under the licence which may facilitate the withdrawal or recall from sale of medicinal products in accordance with paragraph (b);

(b) maintain an emergency plan to ensure effective implementation of the recall from the market of a medicinal product where recall is:

(i) ordered by the licensing authority or by the competent authority of any EEA State, or

(ii) carried out in co-operation with the manufacturer of, or the holder of the marketing authorisation, Article 126a authorisation, certificate of registration or traditional herbal registration for, the product; and

(c) keep records in relation to the receipt, dispatch or brokering of medicinal products, of:

(i) the date of receipt,

(ii) the date of despatch,

(iii) the date of brokering,

(iv) the name of the medicinal product,

(v) the quantity of the product received, dispatched or brokered,

(vi) the name and address of the person from whom the products were received or to whom they are dispatched,

(vii) the batch number of medicinal products bearing safety features referred to in point (o) of Article 54[2] of the 2001 Directive.

(8) A licence holder ("L") who imports from another EEA State a medicinal product in relation to which L is not the holder of a

---

[2] Point (o) of Article 54a was inserted by Directive 2011/62/EU of the European Parliament and of the Council (OJ No L 174, 1.7.2011, p74).

marketing authorisation, Article 126a authorisation, certificate of registration or a traditional herbal registration shall:

(a) notify the intention to import that product to the holder of the authorisation and:

    (i)   in the case of a product which has been granted a marketing authorisation under Regulation (EC) No 726/2004, to the EMA; or

    (ii)   in any other case, the licensing authority; and

(b) pay a fee to the EMA in accordance with Article 76(4)[3] of the 2001 Directive or the licensing authority as the case may be, in accordance with the Fees Regulations, but this paragraph does not apply in relation to the wholesale distribution of medicinal products to a person in a third country.

(9) For the purposes of enabling the licensing authority to determine whether there are grounds for suspending, revoking or varying the licence, the licence holder must permit a person authorised in writing by the licensing authority, on production of identification, to carry out any inspection, or to take any samples or copies, which an inspector could carry out or take under Part 16 (enforcement).

(10) The holder ("L") must verify in accordance with paragraph (11) that any medicinal products received by L that are required by Article 54a[4] of the Directive to bear safety features are not falsified but this paragraph does not apply in relation to the distribution of medicinal products received from a third country by a person to a person in a third country.

(11) Verification under this paragraph is carried out by checking the safety features on the outer packaging, in accordance with the requirements laid down in the delegated acts adopted under Article 54a(2) of the 2001 Directive.

(12) The licence holder must maintain a quality system setting out responsibilities, processes and risk management measures in relation to their activities.

(13) The licence holder must immediately inform the licensing authority and, where applicable, the marketing authorisation holder, of medicinal products which the licence holder receives or is offered which the licence holder:

(a) knows or suspects; or

(b) has reasonable grounds for knowing or suspecting, to be falsified.

---

[3] Article 76(4) was inserted by Directive 2011/62/EU of the European Parliament and of the Council (OJ No L 174, 1.7.2011, p74).

[4] Article 54a was inserted by Directive 2011/62/EU of the European Parliament and of the Council (OJ No L 174, 1.7.2011, p74).

(14) Where the medicinal product is obtained through brokering, the licence holder must verify that the broker involved fulfils the requirements set out in regulation 45A(1)(b).

(15) In this regulation, "marketing authorisation" means:

(a) a marketing authorisation issued by a competent authority in accordance with the 2001 Directive; or

(b) an EU marketing authorisation.

Requirement that wholesale dealers to deal only with specified persons

44   (1)   Unless paragraph (2) applies, the licence holder must not obtain supplies of medicinal products from anyone except:

(a) the holder of a manufacturer's licence or wholesale dealer's licence in relation to products of that description;

(b) the person who holds an authorisation granted by another EEA State authorising the manufacture of products of the description or their distribution by way of wholesale dealing; or

(c) where the supplier is not the holder of a manufacturer's licence, where the supply is in accordance with the principles and guidelines of good distribution practice,

but this paragraph does not apply in relation to the distribution of medicinal products directly received from a third country but not imported into the EU.

(2)   From 28th October 2013 the licence holder must not obtain supplies of medicinal products from anyone except:

(a) the holder of a manufacturer's licence or wholesale dealer's licence in relation to products of that description;

(b) the person who holds an authorisation granted by another EEA State authorising the manufacture of products of the description or their distribution by way of wholesale dealing;

(c) where the medicinal product is directly received from a third country ("A") for export to a third country ("B"), the supplier of the medicinal product in country A is a person who is authorised or entitled to supply such medicinal products in accordance with the legal and administrative provisions in country A; or

(d) where the supplier is not the holder of a manufacturer's licence, where the supply is in accordance with the principles and guidelines of good distribution practice.

(3)   Where a medicinal product is obtained in accordance with paragraph (1), (2)(a) or (b), the licence holder must verify that:

(a) the wholesale dealer who supplies the product complies with the principles and guidelines of good distribution practices; or

(b) the manufacturer or importer who supplies the product holds a manufacturing authorisation.

(4) Unless paragraph (5) applies, the licence holder may distribute medicinal products by way of wholesale dealing only to:

(a) the holder of a wholesale dealer's licence relating to those products;

(b) the holder of an authorisation granted by the competent authority of another EEA State authorising the supply of those products by way of wholesale dealing;

(c) a person who may lawfully sell those products by retail or may lawfully supply them in circumstances corresponding to retail sale; or

(d) a person who may lawfully administer those products,

but this paragraph does not apply in relation to medicinal products which are distributed by way of wholesale dealing to a person in a third country.

(5) From 28th October 2013, the licence holder may distribute medicinal products by way of wholesale dealing only to:

(a) the holder of a wholesale dealer's licence relating to those products;

(b) the holder of an authorisation granted by the competent authority of another EEA State authorising the supply of those products by way of wholesale dealing;

(c) a person who may lawfully sell those products by retail or may lawfully supply them in circumstances corresponding to retail sale;

(d) a person who may lawfully administer those products; or

(e) in relation to supply to persons in third countries, a person who is authorised or entitled to receive medicinal products for wholesale distribution or supply to the public in accordance with the applicable legal and administrative provisions of the third country concerned.

(6) Where a medicinal product is supplied to a person who is authorised or entitled to supply medicinal products to the public in accordance with paragraph (4)(c), (5)(c) or (e), the licence holder must enclose with the product a document stating the:

(a) date on which the supply took place;

(b) name and pharmaceutical form of the product supplied;

(c) quantity of product supplied;

(d) name and address of the licence holder; and

(e) batch number of the medicinal products bearing the safety features referred to in point (o) of Article 54 of the 2001 Directive.

(7)   The licence holder must:

(a) keep a record of information supplied in accordance with paragraph (6) for at least five years beginning immediately after the date on which the information is supplied; and

(b) ensure that the record is available to the licensing authority for inspection.

Requirement as to responsible persons

45   (1)   The licence holder must ensure that there is available at all times at least one person (referred to in this regulation as the "responsible person") who in the opinion of the licensing authority:

(a) has knowledge of the activities to be carried out and of the procedures to be performed under the licence which is adequate to carry out the functions mentioned in paragraph (2); and

(b) has adequate experience relating to those activities and procedures.

(2)   Those functions are:

(a) ensuring that the conditions under which the licence was granted have been, and are being, complied with; and

(b) ensuring that the quality of medicinal products handled by the licence holder is being maintained in accordance with the requirements of the marketing authorisations, Article 126a authorisations, certificates of registration or traditional herbal registrations applicable to those products.

(3)   The licence holder must notify the licensing authority of:

(a) any change to the responsible person; and

(b) the name, address, qualifications and experience of the responsible person.

(4)   The licence holder must not permit any person to act as a responsible person other than the person named in the licence or another person notified to the licensing authority under paragraph (3).

(5)   Paragraph (6) applies if, after giving the licence holder and a person acting as a responsible person the opportunity to make representations (orally or in writing), the licensing authority thinks that the person:

(a) does not satisfy the requirements of paragraph (1) in relation to qualifications or experience; or

(b) is failing to carry out the functions referred to in paragraph (2) adequately or at all.

(6)   Where this paragraph applies, the licensing authority must notify the licence holder in writing that the person is not permitted to act as a responsible person.

Standard provisions of licences

24 (1) The standard provisions set out in Schedule 4 may be incorporated by the licensing authority in a licence under this Part granted on or after the date on which these Regulations come into force.

(2) The standard provisions may be incorporated in a licence with or without modifications and either generally or in relation to medicinal products of a particular class.

Schedule 4 Standard provisions of licences

PART 4 WHOLESALE DEALER'S LICENCE

All wholesale dealer's licences

28 The provisions of this Part are standard provisions of a wholesale dealer's licence.

29 The licence holder must not use any premises for the handling, storage or distribution of medicinal products other than those specified in the licence or notified to the licensing authority from time to time and approved by the licensing authority.

30 The licence holder must provide such information as may be requested by the licensing authority concerning the type and quantity of medicinal products which the licence holder handles, stores or distributes.

31 The licence holder must take all reasonable precautions and exercise all due diligence to ensure that any information provided by the licence holder to the licensing authority which is relevant to an evaluation of the safety, quality or efficacy of a medicinal product which the licence holder handles, stores or distributes is not false or misleading.

Wholesale dealer's licence relating to special medicinal products

32 The provisions of paragraphs 33 to 42 are incorporated as additional standard provisions of a wholesale dealer's licence relating to special medicinal products.

33 Where and in so far as the licence relates to special medicinal products, the licence holder may only import such products from another EEA State:

(a) in response to an order which satisfies the requirements of regulation 167, and

(b) where the conditions set out in paragraphs 34 to 41 are complied with.

34   No later than 28 days prior to each importation of a special medicinal product, the licence holder must give written notice to the licensing authority stating the intention to import the product and stating the following particulars:

(a) the brand name, common name or scientific name of the medicinal product and (if different) any name under which the medicinal product is to be sold or supplied in the United Kingdom;

(b) any trademark or the name of the manufacturer of the medicinal product;

(c) in respect of each active constituent of the medicinal product, any international non-proprietary name or the British approved name or the monograph name, or where that constituent does not have any of those, the accepted scientific name or any other name descriptive of the true nature of the constituent;

(d) the quantity of medicinal product to be imported, which must not exceed the quantity specified in paragraph 38; and

(e) the name and address of the manufacturer or assembler of the medicinal product in the form in which it is to be imported and, if the person who will supply the medicinal product for importation is not the manufacturer or assembler, the name and address of the supplier.

35   The licence holder may not import the special medicinal product if, before the end of 28 days beginning immediately after the date on which the licensing authority sends or gives the licence holder an acknowledgement in writing by the licensing authority that it has received the notice referred to in paragraph 34, the licensing authority has notified the licence holder in writing that the product should not be imported.

36   The licence holder may import the special medicinal product referred to in the notice where the licence holder has been notified in writing by the licensing authority, before the end of the 28-day period referred to in paragraph 35, that the product may be imported.

37   Where the licence holder sells or supplies special medicinal products, the licence holder must, in addition to any other records which are required by the provisions of the licence, make and maintain written records relating to:

(a) the batch number of the batch of the product from which the sale or supply was made; and

(b) details of any adverse reaction to the product sold or supplied of which the licence holder becomes aware.

38   The licence holder must not, on any one occasion, import more than such amount as is sufficient for 25 single administrations, or for 25 courses of

treatment where the amount imported is sufficient for a maximum of three months' treatment, and must not, on any one occasion, import more than the quantity notified to the licensing authority under paragraph 34(d).

39   The licence holder must inform the licensing authority immediately of any matter coming to the licence holder's attention which might reasonably cause the licensing authority to believe that a special medicinal product imported in accordance with this paragraph can no longer be regarded as a product which can safely be administered to human beings or as a product which is of satisfactory quality for such administration.

40   The licence holder must not publish any advertisement, catalogue, or circular relating to a special medicinal product or make any representations in respect of that product.

41   The licence holder must cease importing or supplying a special medicinal product if the licence holder receives a notice in writing from the licensing authority directing that, from a date specified in the notice, a particular product or class of products may no longer be imported or supplied.

42   In this Part:

   "British approved name" means the name which appears in the current edition of the list prepared by the British Pharmacopoeia Commission under regulation 318 (British Pharmacopoeia- lists of names);
   "international non-proprietary name" means a name which has been selected by the World Health Organisation as a recommended international non-proprietary name and in respect of which the Director-General of the World Health Organisation has given notice to that effect in the World Health Organisation Chronicle; and
   "monograph name" means the name or approved synonym which appears at the head of a monograph in the current edition of the British Pharmacopoeia, the European Pharmacopoeia or a foreign or international compendium of standards, and "current" in this definition means current at the time the notice is sent to the licensing authority.

Wholesale dealer's licence relating to exempt advanced therapy medicinal products

43   The provisions of paragraph 44 are incorporated as additional standard provisions of a wholesale dealer's licence relating to exempt advanced therapy medicinal products.

44   The licence holder shall keep the data referred to in paragraph 16 of Schedule 6 for such period, being a period of longer than 30 years, as may be specified by the licensing authority.

Schedule 6 Manufacturer's and wholesale dealer's licences for exempt advanced therapy medicinal products

PART 2 WHOLESALE DEALER'S LICENCES

13   The requirements in paragraphs 14 to 20 apply to a wholesale dealer's licence insofar as it relates to exempt advanced therapy medicinal products.

14   The licence holder must obtain supplies of exempt advanced therapy medicinal products only from:

(a) the holder of a manufacturer's licence in respect of those products; or
(b) the holder of a wholesale dealer's licence in respect of those products.

15   The licence holder must distribute an exempt advanced therapy medicinal product by way of wholesale dealing only to:

(a) the holder of a wholesale dealer's licence in respect of those products; or
(b) a person who:
    (i)   may lawfully administer those products, and
    (ii)   solicited the product for an individual patient.

16   The licence holder must establish and maintain a system ensuring that the exempt advanced therapy medicinal product and its starting and raw materials, including all substances coming into contact with the cells or tissues it may contain, can be traced through the sourcing, manufacturing, packaging, storage, transport and delivery to the establishment where the product is used.

17   The licence holder must inform the licensing authority of any adverse reaction to any exempt advanced therapy medicinal product supplied by the holder of the wholesale dealer's licence of which the holder is aware.

18   The licence holder must, subject to paragraph 44 of Schedule 4, keep the data referred to in paragraph 16 for a minimum of 30 years after the expiry date of the exempt advanced therapy medicinal product.

19   The licence holder must secure that the data referred to in paragraph 16 will, in the event that:

(a) the licence is suspended, revoked or withdrawn; or
(b) the licence holder becomes bankrupt or insolvent,

be held available to the licensing authority by the holder of a wholesale dealer's licence for the period described in paragraph 18 or such longer period as may be required pursuant to paragraph 44 of Schedule 4.

20 The licence holder must not import or export any exempt advanced therapy medicinal product.

UK Legislation on Brokering Medicines

Contents

The Human Medicines Regulations 2012 [SI 2012/1916]

Editor's note   These extracts from the Human Medicines Regulations 2012 [SI 2012/1916] as amended by the Human Medicines (Amendment) Regulations 2013 [SI 2013/1855] are presented for the reader's convenience. Reproduction is with the permission of HMSO and the Queen's Printer for Scotland. For any definitive information reference must be made to the original amending Regulations. The numbering and content within this section corresponds with the regulations set out in the published Statutory Instrument (SI 2012 No. 1916) as amended.

Citation and commencement

1 (1) These Regulations may be cited as the Human Medicines Regulations 2012.

(2) These Regulations come into force on 14th August 2012.

General interpretation

8 (1) In these Regulations (unless the context otherwise requires)-
    "brokering" means all activities in relation to the sale or purchase of medicinal products, except for wholesale distribution, that do not

include physical handling and that consist of negotiating independently and on behalf of another legal or natural person;

"falsified medicinal product" means any medicinal product with a false representation of:

(a) its identity, including its packaging and labelling, its name or its composition (other than any unintentional quality defect) as regards any of its ingredients including excipients and the strength of those ingredients;

(b) its source, including its manufacturer, its country of manufacturing, its country of origin or its marketing authorisation holder; or

(c) its history, including the records and documents relating to the distribution channels used.

Brokering in medicinal products

45A. (1) A person may not broker a medicinal product unless:

    (a) that product is covered by an authorisation granted:

        (i)   under Regulation (EC) No 726/2004; or

        (ii) by a competent authority of a member State; and

    (b) that person:

        (i)   is validly registered as a broker with a competent authority of a member State,

        (ii) except where the person is validly registered with the competent authority of another EEA state, has a permanent address in the United Kingdom, and

        (iii) complies with the guidelines on good distribution practice published by the European Commission in accordance with Article 84 of the 2001 Directive insofar as those guidelines apply to brokers.

  (2) A person is not validly registered for the purpose of paragraph (1)(b) if:

    (a) the person's permanent address is not entered into a register of brokers kept by a competent authority of a member State;

    (b) the registration is suspended; or

    (c) the person has notified the competent authority of a member State to remove that person from the register.

  (3) Paragraph (1)(b)(i) does not apply until 20th October 2013 in relation to a person who brokered any medicinal product before 20th August 2013.

Application for brokering registration

45B. (1) The licensing authority may not register a person as a broker unless paragraphs (2) to (7) are complied with.

(2) An application for registration must be made containing:

(a) the name of the person to be registered;

(b) the name under which that person is trading (if different to the name of that person);

(c) that person's:

(i)   permanent address in the United Kingdom,

(ii) e-mail address, and

(iii) telephone number;

(d) a statement of whether the medicinal products to be brokered are:

(i)   prescription only medicines,

(ii) pharmacy medicines, or

(iii) medicines subject to general sale;

(e) an indication of the range of medicinal products to be brokered;

(f) evidence that that person can comply with regulations 45A(1)(b)(iii), 45E(3)(a) to (f) and 45F(1); and

(g) any fee payable in connection with the application in accordance with the Fees Regulations.

(3) Where the address at which the emergency plan, documents or record necessary to comply with regulation 45E(3)(b) to (d) are kept is different from the address notified in accordance with sub-paragraph (2)(c)(i), the application must contain:

(a) that address where the plan or records are to be kept;

(b) the name of a person who can provide access to that address for the purpose of regulation 325 (rights of entry); and

(c) that person's:

(i)   address,

(ii) e-mail address, and

(iii) telephone number.

(4) Unless paragraph (6) applies, the application for registration must:

(a) be in English; and

(b) be signed by the person seeking a brokering registration.

(5) The pages of the application must be serially numbered.

(6) Where the application is made on behalf of the person seeking a brokering registration by another person ("A"), the application must:

(a) contain the name and address of A; and

(b) be signed by A.

Criteria of broker's registration

45E. (1) Registration of a broker is conditional on that broker:
   (a) complying with regulation 45A(1); and
   (b) satisfying:
       (i) the criteria in paragraphs (3), (4) and (7), and
       (ii) such other criteria as the licensing authority considers appropriate and notifies the broker of.
   (2) The criteria referred to in paragraph (1)(b)(ii) may include (but are not limited to) the criteria specified in paragraphs (5) and (6).
   (3) The broker must:
       (a) have a permanent address in the United Kingdom;
       (b) maintain an emergency plan to ensure effective implementation of the recall from the market of a medicinal product where recall is:
           (i) ordered by the licensing authority or by the competent authority of any EEA State, or
           (ii) carried out in co-operation with the manufacturer of, or the holder of the marketing authorisation, for the product;
       (c) keep documents relating to the sale or supply of medicinal products under the licence which may facilitate the withdrawal or recall from sale of medicinal products in accordance with sub-paragraph (b);
       (d) record in relation to the brokering of each medicinal product:
           (i)   the name of the medicinal product,
           (ii) the quantity of the product brokered,
           (iii) the batch number of the medicinal product bearing the safety features referred to in point (o) of Article 54 of the 2001 Directive,
           (iv) the name and address of the:
                 (aa) supplier, or
                 (bb) consignee, and
           (v)   the date on which the sale or purchase of the product is brokered;
       (e) maintain a quality system setting out responsibilities, processes and risk management measures in relation to their activities; and
       (f) keep the documents or record required by sub-paragraph (c) or (d) available to the licensing authority for a period of five years; and
       (g) comply with regulation 45F(1), (2) and (4).
   (4) Where the address at which the plan or records necessary to comply with paragraph (3)(b) to (d) are kept is different from the address notified in accordance with regulation 45B(2)(c)(i), the broker must:
       (a) ensure that the plan or records are kept at an address in the United Kingdom; and
       (b) inform the licensing authority of the address at which the plan or records are kept.

(5) The broker must provide such information as may be requested by the licensing authority concerning the type and quantity of medicinal products brokered within the period specified by the licensing authority.

(6) The broker must take all reasonable precautions and exercise all due diligence to ensure that any information provided by that broker to the licensing authority in accordance with regulation 45F is not false or misleading.

(7) For the purposes of enabling the licensing authority to determine whether there are grounds for suspending, revoking or varying the registration, the broker must permit a person authorised in writing by the licensing authority, on production of identification, to carry out any inspection, or to take any copies, which an inspector may carry out or take under regulations 325 (rights of entry) and 327 (powers of inspection, sampling and seizure).

Provision of information

45F. (1) A broker registered in the UK must immediately inform:
   (a) the licensing authority; and
   (b) where applicable, the marketing authorisation holder, of medicinal products which the broker identifies as, suspects to be, or has reasonable grounds for knowing or suspecting to be, falsified.

(2) On or before the date specified in paragraph (3), a broker who is, or has applied to the licensing authority to become, a registered broker in the United Kingdom must submit a report to the licensing authority, which:
   (a) includes a declaration that the broker has in place an appropriate system to ensure compliance with regulations 45A, 45B and this regulation; and
   (b) details the system which the broker has in place to ensure such compliance.

(3) The date specified for the purposes of this paragraph is:
   (a) in relation to any application made before 31st March 2014, the date of the application; and
   (b) in relation to each subsequent reporting year, 30th April following the end of that year.

(4) The broker must without delay notify the licensing authority of any changes to the matters in respect of which evidence has been supplied in relation to paragraph (2) which might affect compliance with the requirements of this Chapter.

(5) Any report or notification to the licensing authority under paragraph (2) or (4) must be accompanied by the appropriate fee in accordance with the Fees Regulations.

(6) The licensing authority may give a notice to a registered broker requiring that broker to provide information of a kind specified in the notice within the period specified in the notice.

(7) A notice under paragraph (6) may not be given to a registered broker unless it appears to the licensing authority that it is necessary for the licensing authority to consider whether the registration should be varied, suspended or revoked.

(8) A notice under paragraph (6) may specify information which the licensing authority thinks necessary for considering whether the registration should be varied, suspended or revoked.

(9) In paragraph (3)(b), "reporting year" means a period of twelve months ending on 31st March.

Appendix 1

Human and Veterinary Medicines Authorities in Europe

Austria

Austrian Medicines and Medical Devices Agency - Austrian Federal Office for Safety in Health Care
Traisengasse 5
A-1200 Vienna
Austria
Phone +43 50 555 36111
Email BASG-AGESMedizinmarktaufsicht
@ages.at
Website(s) http://www.basg.gv.at

Belgium

DG Enterprise and Industry - F/2 BREY 10/073
Avenue d'Auderghem 45
B - 1049 Brussels
Belgium

Federal Agency for Medicines and Health Products
EUROSTATION
Victor Horta
40 40
1060 Brussels
Belgium
Email welcome@fagg-afmps.be
Website(s) http://www.fagg-afmps.be/en/

Bulgaria

Bulgarian Drug Agency
8, Damyan Gruev Str
1303 Sofia
Bulgaria
Phone +359 2 8903 555
Fax +359 2 8903 434
Email bda@bda.bg
Website(s) http://www.bda.bg

National Veterinary Service
15A, Pencho Slaveiko Blvd
1606 Sofia
Bulgaria
Phone +359 2 915 98 20
Fax +359 2 954 95 93
Email cvo@nvms.government.bg
Website(s) http://www.nvms.government.bg

Croatia

Croatian Agency for Medicinal Products and Medical Devices
Ksaverska c.4
10000 Zagreb
Croatia
Phone +385 1 4884 100
Fax +385 1 4884 110
Email halmed@halmed.hr
Website(s) http://www.halmed.hr

Ministry of Agriculture, Veterinary and Food Safety Directorate
Planinska Street 2a
10000 Zagreb
Croatia
Phone +385 6443 540
Fax +385 6443 899
Email veterinarstvo@mps.hr
Website(s) http://www.veterinarstvo.hr

Cyprus

Ministry of Health Pharmaceutical Services
7 Larnacos Ave
CY - 1475 Nicosia
Cyprus
Website(s) http://www.moh.gov.cy

Czech Republic

State Institute for Drug Control
Srobárova 48
CZ - 100 41 Praha 10
Czech Republic
Phone + 420 272 185 111
Fax + 420 271 732 377
Email posta@sukl.cz
Website(s) http://www.sukl.eu

**Institute for State Control of Veterinary
Biologicals and Medicaments**
Hudcova Str. 56A
CZ-621 00 Brno-Medlánky
Czech Republic
Phone +420 541 518 211
Fax +420 541 210 026
Email uskvbl@uskvbl.cz
Website(s) http://www.uskvbl.cz/

Denmark

Danish Health and Medicines Agency
Axel Heides Gade 1
DK–2300 København S
Denmark
Phone +45 72 22 74 00
Fax +45 44 88 95 99
Email sst@sst.dk
Website(s) http://www.dkma.dk

European Commission

DG Enterprise F2 Pharmaceuticals
Rue de la Loi 200
B-1049 Brussels
Belgium

**DG Health and Consumers: Unit D6: Medicinal
Products - Quality, Safety and Efficacy; Unit D5:
Medicinal Products - Authorisations, European
Medicines Agency**
Rue de la Loi 200
B-1049 Brussels
Belgium
Phone +32 2 299 11 11
Email: sanco-pharmaceuticals-d5@ec.europa.
eu; sanco-pharmaceuticals-d6@ec.europa.eu
Website(s) http://ec.europa.eu/health/human-
use/index_en.htm

European Medicines Agency (EMA)
7 Westferry Circus
London E14 4HB
United Kingdom
Phone +44 20 74 18 84 00
Fax +44 20 74 18 84 16
Email info@ema.europa.eu
Website(s) http://www.ema.europa.eu/

Estonia

State Agency of Medicines
1 Nooruse St
EE-50411 Tartu
Estonia
Phone +372 737 41 40
Fax +372 737 41 42
Email sam@sam.ee
Website(s) http://www.sam.ee/

Finland

Finnish Medicines Agency
PO Box 55
FI-00034 Fimea
Finland
Phone +358 29 522 3341
Fax +358 29 522 3001
Website(s) http://www.fimea.fi/

France

**French National Agency for Medicines and
Health Products Safety (ANSM)**
143-147 bd
Anatole France
FR-93285 Saint Denis Cedex
France
Email ANSM@ansm.sante.fr
Website(s) http://www.ansm.sante.fr

**Agence Nationale du Médicament Vétérinaire,
Agence nationale de sécurité sanitaire de l'ali-
mentation, de l'environnement et du travail
(ANMV)**
8 rue Claude Bourgelat, Parc d'Activités de la
Grande Marche, Javené BP
CS 70611 - 35306 Fougères
France
Phone +33 (0) 2 99 94 78 71

HUMAN AND VETERINARY
MEDICINES AUTHORITIES
IN EUROPE

Email sylvie.goby@anses.fr
Website(s) http://www.anses.fr

Germany

Federal Institute for Drugs and Medical Devices (BfArM)
Kurt-Georg-Kiesinger-Allee 3
53175 Bonn
Germany
Phone +49 (0)228-207-30
Fax +49 (0)228-207-5207
Email poststelle@bfarm.de
Website(s) http://www.bfarm.de

Federal Office of Consumer Protection and Food Safety
Mauerstraße 39-42
D-10117 Berlin
Germany
Phone +49 30 1 84 44-000
Fax +49 30 1 84 44-89 999
Email poststelle@bvl.bund.de
Website(s) http://www.bvl.bund.de
(pharmaceuticals)

Paul-Ehrlich Institut (Federal Institute for Vaccines and Biomedicines)
Paul-Ehrlich-Straße 51-59
63225 Langen
Germany
Phone +49 6103 77 0
Fax +49 6103 77 1234
Email pei@pei.de
Website(s) http://www.pei.de
(vaccines, blood products, sera)

Greece

National Organization for Medicines
Messogion Avenue 284
GR - 15562 Athens
Greece
Phone +30 210 6507200
Fax +30 210 6545535
Email relation@eof.gr
Website(s) http://www.eof.gr/
(pharmaceuticals and immunologicals)

Hungary

National Institute of Pharmacy
Zrínyi U. 3
H-1051 Budapest
Hungary
Website(s) http://www.ogyi.hu/

National Food Chain Safety Office, Directorate of Veterinary Medicinal Products
Szállás utca 8
H-1107 Budapest 10.Pf. 318
Hungary
Phone +36 1 433 03 30
Fax +36 1 262 28 39
Email info.aogyti@oai.hu
Website(s) http://www.nebih.gov.hu/en/specialities/veterinary

Iceland

Icelandic Medicines Agency
Vinlandsleid 14
IS - 113 Reykjavik
Iceland
Phone +354 520 2100
Fax +354 561 2170
Email ima@ima.is
Website(s) http://www.ima.is

Ireland

Health Products Regulatory Agency
Kevin O'Malley House
Earlsfort Centre
Earlsfort Terrace
IRL - Dublin 2
Ireland
Phone +353 1 676 4971
Fax +353 1 676 7836
Email info@hpra.ie
Website(s) http://www.hpra.ie

Department of Agriculture and Food
Kildare St
Dublin
Ireland
Phone +353 1 607 20 00
Fax +353 1 661 62 63
Email info@agriculture.gov.ie
Website(s) http://www.agriculture.gov.ie

Italy

Italian Medicines Agency
Via del Tritone, 181
I-00187 Rome
Italy
Phone +39 6 5978401
Website(s) http://www.agenziafarmaco.it/

Laboratorio di Medicina Veterinaria, Istituto Superiore di Sanità
Viale Regina Elena 299
I - 00161 Rome
Italy
Phone +39 6 49 38 70 76
Fax +39 6 49 38 70 77

Ministero della Salute, Direzione Generale della Sanità Pubblica Veterinaria, degli Allimenti e della Nutrizione, Uff. XI
Piazzale G. Marconi 25
I - 00144 Rome
Italy
Phone +39 06 59 94 65 84
Fax +39 06 59 94 69 49
Website(s) http://www.ministerosalute.it/

Latvia

State Agency of Medicines of Latvia
15 Jersikas Street
LV - 1003 Riga
Latvia
Phone +371-7078424
Fax +371-7078428
Email info@zva.gov.lv
Website(s) http://www.zva.gov.lv/

Food and Veterinary Service
Peldu St 30
LV - 1050 Riga
Latvia
Phone +371 67095271
Fax +371 67095270
Email nrd@pvd.gov.lv
Website(s) http://www.pvd.gov.lv

Liechtenstein

Office of Health/Medicinal Products Control Agency
Äulestr 512
FL - 9490 Vaduz

Liechtenstein
Email pharminfo@llv.li
Website(s) www.llv.li/

Lithuania

State Medicines Control Agency
Žirmūnų str. 139A
LT-09120 Vilnius
Lithuania
Phone +370 5 263 92 64
Fax +370 5 263 92 65
Email vvkt@vvkt.lt
Website(s) http://www.vvkt.lt/

National Food and Veterinary Risk Assessment Institute
J. Kairiukscio str. 10
LT-08409 Vilnius
Lithuania
Phone +370 5 2780470
Fax +370 5 2780471
Email nmvrvi@vet.lt
Website(s) http://www.nmvrvi.lt

State Food and Veterinary Service
Siesiku str. 19
LT-07170 Vilnius
Lithuania
Email vvt@vet.lt
Website(s) http://www.vet.lt

Luxembourg

Ministry of Health
Allée Marconi
L - 2120 Luxembourg
Luxembourg
Phone +352 24785593
Fax +352 24795615
Email jacqueline.genoux-hames@ms.etat.lu
Website(s) http://www.ms.etat.lu

Malta

Medicines Authority
203, Level 3, Rue D'Argens
GZR 1368 Gzira
Malta

Phone +356 23439000
Fax +356 23439161
Email info.medicinesauthority@gov.mt
Website(s) http://www.medicinesauthority.
gov.mt

Veterinary Medicines and Animal Nutrition Section
Abattoir Square
Albert Town
MRS 1123 Marsa
Malta
Phone + 356 22925375
Email vafd.msdec@gov.mt
Website(s) http://vafd.gov.mt/approved-vet-pharmaceaticals-in-malta

Netherlands

Medicines Evaluation Board
Graadt van Roggenweg 500
NL - 3531 AH Utrecht
The Netherlands
Phone +31 (0) 88 - 224 80 00
Fax +31 (0) 88 - 224 80 01
Website(s) http://www.cbg-meb.nl/

Norway

Norwegian Medicines Agency (NOMA)
Sven Oftedalsvei 6
N - 0950 Oslo
Norway
Phone +47 22 89 77 00
Fax +47 22 89 77 99
Email post@legemiddelverket.no
Website(s) http://www.legemiddelverket.no

Poland

Office for Registration of Medicinal Products, Medical Devices and Biocidal Products
41 Zabkowska Str
03-736 Warsaw
Poland
Phone +48 (22) 492 11 00
Fax +48 (22) 492 11 09
Website(s) http://bip.urpl.gov.pl

Portugal

INFARMED - National Authority of Medicines and Health Products, IP
Av. do Brasil 53
P - 1749-004 Lisbon
Portugal
Phone +351 217987100
Fax +351 217987316
Email infarmed@infarmed.pt
Website(s) http://www.infarmed.pt/portal/page/portal/INFARMED

Food and Veterinary Directorate General
Largo da Academia Nacional de Belas Artes, n. 2
1294-105 Lisbon
Portugal
Phone +351 21 323 95 00
Fax +351 21 346 35 18
Email dirgeral@dgav.pt
Website(s) http://www.dgav.pt

Romania

National Agency for Medicines and Medical Devices
48, Av. Sanatescu
011478 Bucharest
Romania
Phone +4021 3171100
Fax +4021 3163497
Website(s) http://www.anm.ro/en/home.html

Institute for Control of Biological Products and Veterinary Medicines
Str. Dudului 37, sector 6
060603 Bucharest
Romania
Phone +40 21 220 21 12
Fax +40 21 221 31 71
Email icbmv@icbmv.ro
Website(s) http://www.icbmv.ro/

Slovakia

State Institute for Drug Control
Kvetná 11
SK-825 08 Bratislava 26
Slovakia
Phone +421 2 5070 1111
Fax +421 2 5556 4127

mail sukl@sukl.sk
Website(s) http://www.sukl.sk/

**nstitute for State Control of Veterinary Biolo-
icals and Medicaments**
iovetská 34
O Box 52c
K-949 01 Nitra
lovakia
hone +421 37 6515506
ax +421 37 6517915
mail uskvbl@uskvbl.sk
Website(s) http://www.uskvbl.sk/

lovenia

avna agencija Republike Slovenije za zdravila
a medicinske pripomočke
tujska ulica 21
-1000 Ljubljana
lovenia
hone + 38 6 8 2000 500
ax + 38 6 8 2000 510
mail info@jazmp.si
Website(s) http://www.jazmp.si

pain

**panish Agency of Medicines and Medical
evices**
arque Empresarial Las
Mercedes Edificio 8C/
ampezo, 1
- 28022 Madrid
pain
hone +34 91 8225997
ax +34 91 8225128

Email internacional@aemps.es
Website(s) www.agemed.es

Sweden

Medical Products Agency
Dag Hammarskjölds väg 42 / Box 26
SE - 751 03 Uppsala
Sweden
Phone +46 (0) 18 17 46 00
Fax +46 (0) 18 54 85 66
Email registrator@mpa.se
Website(s) www.lakemedelsverket.se

United Kingdom

**Medicines and Healthcare Products Regulatory
Agency**
151 Buckingham Palace Road
Victoria
London
SW1W 9SZ
United Kingdom
Phone +44 (0)20 3080 6000
Fax +44 (0)203 118 9803
Website(s) www.mhra.gov.uk

Veterinary Medicines Directorate (VMD)
Woodham Lane
New Haw
Addlestone
KT15 3LS
United Kingdom
Phone +44 1932 33 69 11
Fax +44 1932 33 66 18
Email postmaster@vmd.defra.gsi.gov.uk
Website(s) www.vmd.defra.gov.uk

HUMAN AND VETERINARY
MEDICINES AUTHORITIES
IN EUROPE

Appendix 2

List of Persons who can be Supplied with Medicines by Way of Wholesale Dealing (Human Medicines Regulations 2012)

Contents

All Medicines

- Doctors and dentists[1]
- Persons lawfully conducting a retail pharmacy business within the meaning of section 69 of the Medicines Act 1968
- Holders of wholesale dealer's licences or persons to whom the restrictions imposed by regulation 18(1) of the Human Medicine Regulations do not apply because of an exemption in those Regulation
- Authorities or persons carrying on the business of -
  (a) an independent hospital, independent clinic or independent medica agency, or
  (b) a hospital or health centre which is not an independent hospital c independent clinic
  (c) a nursing home in Northern Ireland
- Ministers of the Crown and Government Departments
- Scottish Ministers
- Welsh Ministers
- Northern Ireland Ministers

---

[1] Health professionals may order medicines using a doctor or dentist's letter c authority. The letter should be clear that the health professional is authorised t order medicines on the doctor or dentist's behalf for delivery to that doctor c dentist.

- A person other than an excepted person (in this context a pharmacist) who carries on a business consisting (wholly or partly) of the supply or administration of medicinal products for the purpose of assisting the provision of health care by or on behalf of, or under arrangements made by -
  (a) a police force in England, Wales or Scotland,
  (b) the Police Service of Northern Ireland,
  (c) a prison service, or
  (d) Her Majesty's Forces.
- A person other than an excepted person (in this context a pharmacist) who carries on a business consisting (wholly or partly) of the supply or administration of medicinal products for the purpose of assisting the provision of health care by or on behalf of, or under arrangements made by –
  (a) NHS trust or NHS foundation trust
  (b) The Common Services Agency
  (c) A local authority in the exercise of public health functions (within the meaning of the NHS Act 2006)
  (d) A health authority or special health authority
  (e) A clinical commissioning group
  (f) NHS England
  (g) A local authority

Pharmacy Medicines

- Pharmacy medicines which are for the purpose of administration in the course of a business can be supplied to a person carrying on that business.

General Sale List Medicines

- Any person who requires GSL medicines for the purpose of selling, supplying or administering them to human beings in the course of a business carried on by that person.

Other Relevant Provisions

- Under medicines legislation, the general rule is that prescription only medicines may only be sold or supplied on a retail basis against a prescription on registered pharmacy premises by or under the supervision of a pharmacist. There are exemptions from these restrictions for certain persons in respect of specific medicines which are contained in Schedule 17 to the Human Medicines Regulations 2012. The Regulations allow people who have exemptions to be sold the prescription only medicines relevant to their particular exemption on a wholesale basis. **See Schedule 17.**

- Similarly, the general rule for pharmacy medicines is that they may only be sold or supplied by or under the supervision of a pharmacist or registered pharmacy premises. Again, there are exemptions from these restrictions for certain persons in respect of specific medicines contained in Schedule 17 of the Human Medicines Regulations 2012 and the Regulations allow for the sale of the P medicines on the same basis as for POMs (above). **See Schedule 17.**

Additional Provisions for Optometrists and Dispensing Opticians not included in Schedule 17

- The Human Medicines Regulations also contain other provisions which allow wholesale sales in certain circumstances:

  (a) Registered optometrists can obtain a range of medicines on a wholesale basis for sale or supply in the course of their professional practice. In addition to these arrangements, they may also obtain prescription only medicines containing the following substances for administration:

     Amethocaine hydrochloride
     Lignocaine hydrochloride
     Oxybuprocaine hydrochloride
     Proxymetacaine hydrochloride

  (b) Additional Supply Optometrists can be sold a product that is only classed as a POM because it contains Thymoxamine Hydrochloride.

  (c) Dispensing opticians can obtain the following which are required for use by a registered optometrist or doctor attending their practice:

     Amethocaine Hydrochloride
     Chloramphenicol
     Cyclopentolate Hydrochloride
     Fusidic Acid
     Lidocaine Hydrochloride
     Oxybuprocaine Hydrochloride
     Proxymetacaine Hydrochloride
     Tropicamide

  (d) Dispensing opticians can also obtain medicines that are required in the course of their professional practice as a contact lens specialist which contain one or more of the following substances:

     Lidocaine Hydrochloride
     Oxybuprocaine Hydrochloride
     Proxymetacaine Hydrochloride

SCHEDULE 17 PROVISIONS

PART 1 Exemption from restrictions on Sale or Supply of Prescription Only Medicines

Persons exempted	Prescription only medicines to which the exemption applies	Conditions
1. Persons selling or supplying prescription only medicines to universities, other institutions concerned with higher education or institutions concerned with research.	1. All prescription only medicines.	1. The sale or supply shall be— (a) subject to the presentation of an order signed by the principal of an institution concerned with educational research or the appropriate head of department in charge of a specified course of research stating— (i) the name of the institution for which the prescription only medicine is required, and (ii) the purpose for which the prescription only medicine is required, and (iii) the total quantity required; and (b) for the purpose of the education or research with which the institution is concerned.
2. Persons selling or supplying prescription only medicines to any of the following— (a) a public analyst appointed under section 27 of the Food Safety Act 1990(1) or article 27 of the Food Safety (Northern Ireland) Order 1991(2); (b) an authorised officer within the meaning of section 5(6) of the Food Safety Act 1990(3); (c) a sampling officer within the meaning of article 38(1) of the Food (Northern Ireland) Order 1989(4); (d) an inspector acting under regulations 325 to 328; (e) a sampling officer within the meaning of Schedule 31.	2. All prescription only medicines.	2. The sale or supply shall be subject to the presentation of an order signed by or on behalf of any person listed in column 1 stating the status of the person signing it and the amount of prescription only medicine required, and shall be only in connection with the exercise by those persons of their statutory functions.

Persons exempted	Prescription only medicines to which the exemption applies	Conditions
3. Persons selling or supplying prescription only medicines to any person employed or engaged in connection with a scheme for testing the quality and checking the amount of the drugs and appliances supplied under the National Health Service Act 2006(5), the National Health Service (Scotland) Act 1978(6), the National Health Service (Wales) Act 2006(7) and the Health and Personal Social Services (Northern Ireland) Order 1972(8), or under any subordinate legislation made under those Acts or that Order.	3. All prescription only medicines	3. The sale or supply shall be— (a) subject to the presentation of an order signed by or on behalf of the person so employed or engaged stating the status of the person signing it and the amount of the prescription only medicine required; and (b) for the purposes of a scheme referred to in column 1 in this paragraph.
4. Registered midwives.	4. Prescription only medicines containing any of the following substances— (a) Diclofenac; (b) Hydrocortisone Acetate; (c) Miconazole; (d) Nystatin; (e) Phytomenadione;	4. The sale or supply shall be only in the course of their professional practice.
5. Persons lawfully conducting a retail pharmacy business within the meaning of section 69 of the Medicines Act 1968.	5. Water for injection.	5. The sale or supply is to a person— (a) for a purpose other than parenteral administration; or (b) who has been prescribed dry powder for parenteral administration but has not been prescribed the water for injection that is needed as a diluent.
6. Persons lawfully conducting a retail pharmacy business within the meaning of section 69 of the Medicines Act 1968.	6. Items which are— (a) prescription only medicines which are not for parenteral administration and which— (i) are eye drops and are prescription only medicines by reason only that they contain not more than 0.5 per cent of Chloramphenicol, or (ii) are eye ointments and are prescription only medicines by reason only that they contain not more than 1.0 per cent Chloramphenicol, or (iii) are prescription only medicines by reason only that they contain any of the following substances—	6. The sale or supply shall be subject to the presentation of an order signed by— (a) a registered optometrist for a medicine listed under item (a) in column 2; (b) a registered chiropodist or podiatrist for a medicine listed under item (b) in column 2.

Persons exempted	Prescription only medicines to which the exemption applies	Conditions
	(aa) Cyclopentolate hydrochloride,	
	(bb) Fusidic Acid,	
	(cc) Tropicamide;	
	(b) the following prescription only medicines—	
	(i) Amorolfine hydrochloride cream where the maximum strength of the Amorolfine in the cream does not exceed 0.25 per cent by weight in weight,	
	(ii) Amorolfine hydrochloride lacquer where the maximum strength of Amorolfine in lacquer does not exceed 5 per cent by weight in volume,	
	(iii) Amoxicillin,	
	(iv) Co-Codamol,	
	(v) Co-dydramol 10/500 tablets,	
	(vi) Codeine Phosphate,	
	(vii) Erythromycin,	
	(viii) Flucloxacillin,	
	(ix) Silver Sulfadiazine,	
	(x) Tioconazole 28%,	
	(xi) Topical hydrocortisone where the maximum strength of hydrocortisone in the medicinal product does not exceed 1 per cent by weight in weight.	
. Registered optometrists.	7. Prescription only medicines listed in item (a) of paragraph 6 column 2.	7. The sale or supply shall be only— (a) in the course of their professional practice, and (b) in an emergency.
. Persons lawfully conducting a retail pharmacy business within the meaning of section 69 of the Medicines Act 1968.	8. Medicinal products not for parenteral administration which are prescription only medicines by reason only that they contain any of the following substances— (a) Acetylcysteine, (b) Atropine sulphate,	8. The sale or supply shall be subject to the presentation of an order signed by an additional supply optometrist.

Persons exempted	Prescription only medicines to which the exemption applies	Conditions
	(c) Azelastine hydrochloride,	
	(d) Diclofenac sodium,	
	(e) Emedastine,	
	(f) Homotropine hydrobromide,	
	(g) Ketotifen,	
	(h) Levocabastine,	
	(i) Lodoxamide,	
	(j) Nedocromil sodium,	
	(k) Olopatadine,	
	(l) Pilocarpine hydrochloride,	
	(m) Pilocarpine nitrate,	
	(n) Polymyxin B/bacitracin,	
	(o) Polymyxin B/trimethoprim,	
	(p) Sodium cromoglycate.	
9. Additional supply optometrists.	9. Prescription only medicines specified in paragraph 8 column 2.	9. The sale or supply shall be only— (a) in the course of their professional practice, and (b) in an emergency.
10. Holders of marketing authorisations, product licences or manufacturer's licences.	10. Prescription only medicines referred to in those authorisations or licences.	10. The sale or supply shall be only— (a) to a pharmacist, (b) so as to enable that pharmacist to prepare an entry relating to the prescription only medicine in question in a tablet or capsule identification guide or similar publication, and (c) of no greater quantity than is reasonably necessary for that purpose.
11. Registered chiropodists or podiatrists against whose names are recorded in the relevant register annotations signifying that they are qualified to use the medicine specified in column 2.	11. The following prescription only medicines— (a) Amorolfine hydrochloride cream where the maximum strength of the Amorolfine in the cream does not exceed 0.25 per cent by weight in weight, (b) Amorolfine hydrochloride lacquer where the maximum strength of Amorolfine in lacquer does not exceed 5 per cent by weight in volume, (c) Amoxicillin, (d) Co-Codamol, (e) Co-dydramol 10/500 tablets, (f) Codeine Phosphate,	11. The sale or supply shall be only in the course of their professional practice.

Persons exempted	Prescription only medicines to which the exemption applies	Conditions
	(g) Erythromycin,	
	(h) Flucloxacillin,	
	(i) Silver Sulfadiazine,	
	(j) Tioconazole 28%,	
	(k) Topical hydrocortisone where the maximum strength of hydrocortisone in the medicinal product does not exceed 1 per cent by weight in weight.	
12. Persons selling or supplying prescription only medicines to a school.	12. A prescription only medicinal product comprising an inhaler containing salbutamol.	12. The sale or supply shall be— (a) subject to the presentation of an order signed by the principal or head teacher at the school concerned stating— (i) the name of the school for which the medicinal product is required, (ii) the purpose for which that product is required, and (iii) the total quantity required, and (b) for the purpose of supplying the medicinal product to pupils at the school in an emergency.

PART 2 Exemption from the restriction on supply of prescription only medicines

Persons exempted	Prescription only medicines to which the exemption applies	Conditions
1. Royal National Lifeboat Institution and certified first aiders of the Institution.	1. All prescription only medicines	1. The supply shall be only so far as is necessary for the treatment of sick or injured persons in the exercise of the functions of the Institution.
2. The owner or master of a ship which does not carry a doctor on board as part of the ship's complement.	2. All prescription only medicines.	2. The supply shall be only so far as is necessary for the treatment of persons on the ship.
3. Persons authorised by licences granted under regulation 5 of the Misuse of Drugs Regulations 2001(**9**) or regulation 5 of the Misuse of Drugs Regulations (Northern Ireland) 2002(**10**) to supply a controlled drug.	3. Such prescription only medicines, being controlled drugs, as are specified in the licence.	3. The supply shall be subject to such conditions and in such circumstances and to such an extent as may be specified in the licence.
4. Persons employed or engaged in the provision of lawful drug treatment services.	4. Ampoules of sterile water for injection that contain no more than 2ml of water each.	4. The supply shall be only in the course of provisions of lawful drug treatment services.
5. Persons requiring prescription only medicines for the purpose of enabling them, in the course of any business carried on by them, to comply with any requirements made by or in pursuance of any enactment with respect to the medical treatment of their employees.	5. Such prescription only medicines as may be specified in the relevant enactment.	5. The supply shall be— (a) for the purpose of enabling them to comply with any requirements made by or in pursuance of any such enactment, and (b) subject to such conditions and such circumstances as may be specified in the relevant enactment.

Persons exempted	Prescription only medicines to which the exemption applies	Conditions
6. Persons operating an occupational health scheme.	6. Prescription only medicines sold or supplied to a person operating an occupational health scheme in response to an order in writing signed by a doctor or a registered nurse.	6. The supply of the prescription only medicine shall be— (a) in the course of operating an occupational health scheme, and (b) made by— (i) a doctor, or (ii) a registered nurse acting in accordance with the written directions of a doctor as to the circumstance in which such medicines are to be used in the course of an occupational health scheme.
7. The operator or commander of an aircraft.	7. Prescription only medicines which are not for parenteral administration and which have been sold or supplied to an operator or commander of an aircraft in response to an order in writing signed by a doctor.	7. The supply shall be only so far as is necessary for the immediate treatment of sick or injured persons on the aircraft and shall be in accordance with the written instructions of a doctor as to the circumstances in which prescription only medicines of the description in question are to be used on the aircraft.
8. Persons employed as qualified first-aid personnel on off-shore installations.	8. All prescription only medicines.	8. The supply shall be only so far as is necessary for the treatment of persons on the installation.
9. Persons who hold a certificate in first aid from the Mountain Rescue Council of England and Wales, or from the Northern Ireland Mountain Rescue Co-ordinating Committee.	9. Prescription only medicines supplied to a person specified in column 1 in response to an order in writing signed by a doctor.	9. The supply shall be only so far as is necessary for the treatment of sick or injured persons in the course of providing mountain rescue services.
10. Persons ("P") who are members of Her Majesty's armed forces.	10. All prescription only medicines.	10. The supply shall be— (a) in the course of P undertaking any function as a member of Her Majesty's armed forces; and (b) where P is satisfied that it is not practicable for another person who is legally entitled to supply a prescription only medicine to do so; and (c) only in so far as is necessary— (i) for the treatment of a sick or injured person in a medical emergency, or (ii) to prevent ill-health where there is a risk that a person would suffer ill-health if the prescription only medicine is not supplied.
11. A person ("P") carrying on the business of a school who is trained to administer the relevant medicine.	11. A prescription only medicinal product comprising an inhaler containing salbutamol.	11. The supply shall be— (a) in the course of P carrying on the business of a school; (b) where supply is to a pupil at that school who is known to suffer from asthma; and (c) where the pupil requires the medicinal product in an emergency.

PART 3 Exemptions from the restriction on administration of prescription only medicines

Persons exempted	Prescription only medicines to which the exemption applies	Conditions
1. Registered chiropodists or podiatrists against whose names are recorded in the relevant register annotations signifying that they are qualified to use the medicines specified in column 2.	1. Prescription only medicines for parenteral administration that contain— (a) Adrenaline, (b) Bupivacaine hydrochloride, (c) Bupivacaine hydrochloride with adrenaline where the maximum strength of adrenaline does not exceed 1 mg in 200 ml of bupivacaine hydrochloride, (d) Levobupivacaine hydrochloride, (e) Lidocaine hydrochloride, (f) Lidocaine hydrochloride with adrenaline where the maximum strength of adrenaline does not exceed 1 mg in 200 ml of lignocaine hydrochloride, (g) Mepivacaine hydrochloride, (h) Methylprednisolone, (i) Prilocaine hydrochloride, (j) Ropivacaine hydrochloride.	1. The administration shall only be in the course of their professional practice and where the medicine includes a combination of substances in column 2, those substances shall not have been combined by the chiropodist or podiatrist.
2. Registered midwives and student midwives.	2. Prescription only medicines for parenteral administration containing any of the following substances but no other substance that is classified as a product available on prescription only— (a) Adrenaline, (b) Anti-D immunoglobulin, (c) Carboprost, (d) Cyclizine lactate, (e) Diamorphine, (f) Ergometrine maleate, (g) Gelofusine, (h) Hartmann's solution, (i) Hepatitis B vaccine, (j) Hepatitis immunoglobulin, (k) Lidocaine hydrochloride, (l) Morphine, (m) Naloxone hydrochloride, (n) Oxytocins, natural and synthetic, (o) Pethidine hydrochloride, (p) Phytomenadione, (q) Prochloperazine, (r) Sodium chloride 0.9%.	2. The medicine shall— (a) in the case of Lidocaine and Lidocaine hydrochloride, be administered only while attending on a woman in childbirth, and (b) where administration is— (i) by a registered midwife, be administered in the course of their professional practice; (ii) by a student midwife— (aa) be administered under the direct supervision of a registered midwife; and (bb) not include Diamorphine, Morphine or Pethidine hydrochloride.

Persons exempted	Prescription only medicines to which the exemption applies	Conditions
3. Persons who are authorised as members of a group by a group authority granted under regulations 8(3) or 9(3) of the Misuse of Drugs Regulations 2001(**11**) or, regulations 8(3) or 9(3) of the Misuse of Drugs Regulations (Northern Ireland) 2002(**12**), to supply a controlled drug by way of administration only.	3. Prescription only medicines that are specified in the group authority.	3. The administration shall be subject to such conditions and in such circumstances and to such extent as may be specified in the group authority.
4. The owner or master of a ship which does not carry a doctor on board as part of the ship's complement.	4. All prescription only medicines that are for parenteral administration.	4. The administration shall be only so far as is necessary for the treatment of persons on the ship.
5. Persons operating an occupational health scheme.	5. Prescription only medicines that are for parenteral administration sold or supplied to the person operating an occupational health scheme in response to an order in writing signed by a doctor or a registered nurse.	5. The prescription only is administered in the course of an occupational health scheme, and the individual administering the medicine is— (a) a doctor, or (b) a registered nurse acting in accordance with the written instructions of a doctor as to the circumstances in which prescription only medicines of the description in question are to be used.
6. The operator or commander of an aircraft.	6. Prescription only medicines for parenteral administration which have been sold or supplied to the operator or commander of the aircraft in response to an order in writing signed by a doctor.	6. The administration shall be only so far as is necessary for the immediate treatment of sick or injured persons on the aircraft and shall be in accordance with the written instructions of the doctor as to the circumstances in which prescription only medicines of the description in question are to be used on the aircraft.
7. Persons employed as qualified first-aid personnel on off-shore installations.	7. All prescription only medicines that are for parenteral administration.	7. The administration shall be only so far as is necessary for the treatment of persons on the installation.
8. Persons who are registered paramedics.	8. The following prescription only medicines for parenteral administration— (a) Diazepam 5 mg per ml emulsion for injection, (b) Succinylated Modified Fluid Gelatin 4 per cent intravenous infusion, (c) medicines containing the substance Ergometrine Maleate 500 mcg per ml with Oxytocin 5 iu per ml, but no other active ingredient,	8. The administration shall be only for the immediate, necessary treatment of sick or injured persons and in the case of prescription only medicine containing Heparin Sodium shall be only for the purpose of cannula flushing.

Persons exempted	Prescription only medicines to which the exemption applies	Conditions
	(d) prescription only medicines containing one or more of the following substances, but no other active ingredient—	
	(i) Adrenaline Acid Tartrate,	
	(ii) Adrenaline hydrochloride,	
	(iii) Amiodarone,	
	(iv) Anhydrous glucose,	
	(v) Benzlypenicillin,	
	(vi) Compound Sodium Lactate Intravenous Infusion (Hartmann's Solution),	
	(vii) Ergometrine Maleate,	
	(viii) Furosemide,	
	(ix) Glucose,	
	(x) Heparin Sodium,	
	(xi) Lidocaine Hydrochloride,	
	(xii) Metoclopramide,	
	(xiii) Morphine Sulphate,	
	(xiv) Nalbuphine Hydrochloride,	
	(xv) Naloxone Hydrochloride,	
	(xvi) Ondansetron	
	(xvii) Paracetamol,	
	(xviii) Reteplase,	
	(xix) Sodium Chloride,	
	(xx) Streptokinase,	
	(xxi) Tenecteplase.	
9. Persons who hold the advanced life support provider certificate issued by the Resuscitation Council (UK).	9. The following prescription only medicines for parenteral administration — (a) Adrenaline 1:10,000 up to I mg; and (b) Amiodarone.	9. The administration shall be only in an emergency involving cardiac arrest, and in the case of adrenaline the administration shall be intravenous only.
10. Persons ("P") who are members of Her Majesty's armed forces.	10. All prescription only medicines.	10. The administration shall be— (a) in the course of P undertaking any function as a member of Her Majesty's armed forces; and (b) where P is satisfied that it is not practicable for another person who is legally entitled to administer a prescription only medicine to do so; and (c) only in so far as is necessary— (i) for the treatment of a sick or injured person in an emergency, or (ii) to prevent ill-health where there is a risk that a person would suffer ill-health if the prescription only medicine is not administered.

LIST OF PERSONS WHO CAN BE SUPPLIED WITH MEDICINES

PART 4 Exemptions from the restrictions in regulations 220 and 221 for certain persons who sell, supply, or offer for sale or supply certain medicinal products

Persons exempted	Medicinal products to which exemption applies	Conditions
1. Registered chiropodists and podiatrists.	1. Medicinal products on a general sale list which are for external use and are not veterinary drugs and the following pharmacy medicines for external use— (a) Potassium permanganate crystals or solution; (b)ointment of heparinoid and hyaluronidase; and (c) products containing, as their only active ingredients, any of the following substances, at a strength, in the case of each substance, not exceeding that specified in relation to that substance— (i) 9.0 per cent Borotannic complex (ii) 10.0 per cent Buclosamide (iii) 3.0 per cent Chlorquinaldol (iv) 1.0 per cent Clotrimazole (v) 10.0 per cent Crotamiton (vi) 5.0 per cent Diamthazole hydrochloride (vii) 1.0 per cent Econazole nitrate (viii) 1.0 per cent Fenticlor (ix) 10.0 per cent Glutaraldehyde (x) 1.0 per cent Griseofulvin (xi) 0.4 per cent Hydrargaphen (xii) 2.0 per cent Mepyramine maleate (xiii) 2.0 per cent Miconazole nitrate (xiv) 2.0 per cent Phenoxypropan-2-ol (xv) 20.0 per cent Podophyllum resin (xvi) 10.0 per cent Polynoxylin (xvii) 70.0 per cent Pyrogallol (xviii) 70.0 per cent Salicylic acid (xix) 1.0 per cent Terbinafine (xx) 0.1 per cent Thiomersal.	
2. Registered chiropodists and podiatrists against whose names are recorded in the relevant register annotations signifying that they are qualified to use the medicines in column 2.	2. (a) The following prescription only medicines— (i) Amorolfine hydrochloride cream where the maximum strength of the Amorolfine in the cream does not exceed 0.25 per cent by weight in weight,	2. The sale or supply shall be only in the course of their professional practice, and the medicinal product must have been made up for sale or supply in a container elsewhere than at the place at which it is sold or supplied.

rsons exempted	Medicinal products to which exemption applies	Conditions
	(ii) Amorolfine hydrochloride lacquer where the maximum strength of Amorolfine in the lacquer does not exceed 5 per cent by weight in volume,	
	(iii) Amoxicillin,	
	(iv) Co-Codamol,	
	(v) Co-dydramol 10/500 tablets,	
	(vi) Codeine Phosphate,	
	(vii) Erythromycin,	
	(viii) Flucloxacillin,	
	(ix) Silver Sulfadiazine,	
	(x) Tioconazole 28%, (xi) Topical hydrocortisone where the maximum strength of the hydrocortisone in the medicinal product does not exceed 1 per cent by weight in weight; and	
	(b) Ibuprofen, other than preparations of ibuprofen which are prescription only medicines.	
. Registered optometrists.	3. All medical products on a general sale list, all pharmacy medicines and prescription only medicines which are not for parenteral administration and which—	3. The sale or supply shall be only—
	(a) are eye drops and are prescription only medicines by reason only that they contain not more than—	(a) in the case of medicinal products on a general sale list and pharmacy medicines, in the course of their professional practice;
	(i) 30.0 per cent Sulphacetamide Sodium, or	
	(ii) 0.5 per cent Chloramphenicol, or	(b) in the case of prescription only medicines, in the course of their professional practice and in an emergency.
	(b) are eye ointments and are prescription only medicines by reason only that they contain not more than—	
	(i) 30.0 per cent Sulphacetamide Sodium, or	
	(ii) 1.0 per cent Chloramphenicol, or	
	(c) are prescription only medicines by reason only that they contain any of the following substances—	
	(i) Cyclopentolate hydrochloride,	
	(ii) Fusidic acid,	
	(iii) Tropicamide.	

LIST OF PERSONS WHO CAN BE SUPPLIED WITH MEDICINES

Persons exempted	Medicinal products to which exemption applies	Conditions
4. Additional supply optometrists.	4. Medicinal products which are prescription only medicines by reason only that they contain any of the following substances— (a) Acetylcysteine, (b) Atropine sulphate, (c) Azelastine hydrochloride, (d) Diclofenac sodium, (e) Emedastine, (f) Homotropine hydrobromide, (g) Ketotifen, (h) Levocabastine, (i) Lodoximide, (j) Nedocromil sodium, (k) Olopatadine, (l) Pilocarpine hydrochloride, (m) Pilocarpine nitrate, (n) Polymyxin B/bacitracin, (o) Polymyxin B/trimethoprim, (p) Sodium Cromoglycate.	4. The sale or supply shall be only in the course of their professional practice and only in an emergency.
5. Holders of manufacturer's licences where the licence in question contains a provision that the licence holder shall manufacture the medicinal product to which the licence relates only for a particular person after being requested by or on behalf of that person and in that person's presence to use his own judgement as to the treatment required.	5. Medicinal products on a general sale list which are for external use and are not veterinary drugs and pharmacy medicines which are for external use in the treatment of hair and scalp conditions and which contain any of the following— (a) not more than 5.0 per cent of Boric acid, (b) Isopropyl myristate or Lauryl sulphate, (c) not more than 0.004 per cent Oestrogens, (d) not more than 1.0 per cent of Resorcinol, (e) not more than 3.0 per cent of Salicylic acid, (f) not more than 0.2 per cent of Sodium pyrithione.	5. The licence holder shall sell or supply the medicinal product in question only to a particular person after being requested by or on behalf of that person and in that person's presence to use his own judgement as to the treatment required.
6. Persons selling or supplying medicinal products to universities, other institutions concerned with higher education or institutions concerned with research.	6. All medicinal products.	6. The sale or supply shall be— (a) Subject to the presentation of an order signed by the principal of the institution concerned with education or research or the

Persons exempted	Medicinal products to which exemption applies	Conditions
		appropriate head of department in charge of the specified course of research stating—
		(i) the name of the institution for which the medicinal product is required,
		(ii) the purpose for which the medicinal product is required, and
		(iii) the total quantity required, and
		(b) for the purposes of the education or research with which the institution is concerned.
7. Persons selling or supplying medicinal products to organisations for research purposes.	7. All medicinal products.	7. The sale or supply is only for the purposes of research and shall be—
		(a) subject to the presentation of an order signed by the representative of the organisation concerned stating—
		(i) who requires the medicine,
		(ii) the purposes for which it is required,
		(iii) the quantity required, and
		(iv) the purposes of the research with which the organisation is concerned; and
		(b) not for administration to humans.
8. Persons selling or supplying medicinal products to any of the following— (a) a public analyst appointed under section 27 of the Food Safety Act 1990 or under article 27 of the Food Safety (Northern Ireland) Order 1991; (b) an agricultural analyst appointed under section 67 of the Agriculture Act 1970(**13**), (c) a person duly authorised by an enforcement authority under regulations 325 to 328, (d) a sampling officer within the meaning a sampling officer within the meaning of schedule 31.	8. All medicinal products.	8. The sale or supply is in connection with the exercise of any statutory function carried out by any person listed in sub-paragraphs (a) to (d) of column 1 provided that— (a) the medicinal products are requested on an order signed by or on behalf of a person listed in sub-paragraph (a) to (d) of column 1, and (b) the order gives— (i) the status of the person signing it, (ii) the amount of medicinal product required.

Persons exempted	Medicinal products to which exemption applies	Conditions
9. Holders of a marketing authorisation, a certificate of registration or a manufacturer's licence.	9. Medicinal product referred to in the marketing authorisation, certificate of registration or manufacturer's licence.	The sale or supply shall be only— (a) to a pharmacist, (b) so as to enable that pharmacist to prepare an entry relating to the medical product in question in a tablet or capsule identification guide or similar publication, and (c) of no greater quantity than is reasonably necessary for that purpose.
10. Registered dispensing opticians.	10. Pharmacy medicines for external use containing chloramphenicol at a strength not exceeding— (a) 0.5 per cent in eye drops; (b) 1 per cent in ointment.	10. The sale or supply shall only be in the course of their professional practice.
11. Operator or commander of an aircraft.	11. All medicinal products on a general sale list.	11. The medicinal product must— (a) have been made up for sale or supply in a container elsewhere than at the place at which it is sold or supplied; and (b) be stored in a part of the aircraft which the operator is able to close so as to exclude the public.
12. The operator of a train.	12. All medicinal products on a general sale list.	12. The medicinal product must— (a) have been made up for sale or supply in a container elsewhere than at the place at which it is sold or supplied; and (b) be stored in a part of the train which the operator is able to close so as to exclude the public.

PART 5 Exemptions from the restrictions in regulations 220 and 221 for certain persons who supply certain medicinal products

Persons exempted	Medicinal products to which exemption applies	Conditions
1. Royal National Lifeboat Institution and certificated first aiders of the Institution.	1. All medicinal products.	1. The supply shall be only so far as is necessary for the treatment of sick or injured persons.
2. British Red Cross Society and certificated first aid and certificated nursing members of the Society.	2. All pharmacy medicines and all medicinal products on a general sale list.	2. The supply shall be only so far as is necessary for the treatment of sick or injured persons.
3. St John Ambulance Association and Brigade and certificated first aid and certificated nursing members of the Association and Brigade.	3. All pharmacy medicines and all medicinal products on a general sale list.	3. The supply shall be only so far as is necessary for the treatment of sick or injured persons.

Persons exempted	Medicinal products to which exemption applies	Conditions
St. Andrew's Ambulance Association and certificated first aid and certificated nursing members of the Association.	4. All pharmacy medicines and all medicinal products on a general sale list.	4. The supply shall be only so far as is necessary for the treatment of sick and injured persons.
Order of Malta Ambulance Corps and certificated first aid and certificated nursing members of the Corps.	5. All pharmacy medicines and all medicinal products on a general sale list.	5. The supply shall be only so far as is necessary for the treatment of sick or injured persons.
Persons authorised by licences granted under regulation 5 of the Misuse of Drugs Regulations 2001 or regulation 5 of the Misuse of Drugs Regulations (Northern Ireland) 2002.	6. Such prescription only medicines and such pharmacy medicines as are specified in the licence.	6. The supply shall be subject to such conditions and in such circumstances and to such an extent as may be specified in the licence.
Persons employed or engaged in the provision of lawful drug treatment services.	7. Ampoules of sterile water for injection that contain no more than 5ml of water each.	7. The supply shall be only in the course of provision of lawful drug treatment services.
Persons requiring medicinal products for the purpose of enabling them, in the course of any business carried on by them, to comply with any requirements made by or in pursuance of any enactment with respect to the medical treatment of their employees.	8. Such prescription only medicines and such pharmacy medicines as may be specified in the relevant enactment and medicinal products on a general sale list.	8. The supply shall be— (a) for the purpose of enabling compliance with any requirement made by or in pursuance of any such enactment, and (b) subject to such conditions and in such circumstances as may be specified in the relevant enactment.
The owner or master of a ship which does not carry a doctor on board as part of the ship's complement.	9. All medicinal products.	9. The supply shall be only so far as is necessary for the treatment of persons on the ship.
0. Persons operating an occupational health scheme.	10. All pharmacy medicines, all medicinal products on a general sale list and such prescription only medicines as are sold or supplied to a person operating an occupational health scheme in response to an order signed by a doctor or a registered nurse.	10. (a) The supply shall be in the course of an occupational health scheme. (b) The individual supplying the medicinal product, if not a doctor, shall be— (i) a registered nurse, and (ii) where the medicinal product in question is a prescription only medicine, acting in accordance with the written instructions of a doctor as to the circumstances in which

LIST OF PERSONS WHO CAN BE SUPPLIED WITH MEDICINES

Persons exempted	Medicinal products to which exemption applies	Conditions
		prescription only medicines of the description in question are to be used in the course of an occupational health scheme.
11. Persons carrying on the business of a school providing full-time education.	11. Pharmacy medicines that are for use in the prevention of dental caries and consist of or contain Sodium Fluoride.	11. The supply shall be— (a) in the course of a school dental scheme, and (b) if to a child under 16 only where the parent or guardian of that child has consented to such supply.
12. Health authorities or Primary Health Trusts.	12. Pharmacy medicines that are for use in the prevention of dental caries and consist of or contain Sodium Fluoride.	12. The supply shall be in the course of— (a) a pre-school dental scheme, and the individual supplying the medicinal product shall be a registered nurse, or (b) a school dental scheme, and if to a child under 16 only where the parent or guardian of that child has consented to such supply.
13. The operator or commander of an aircraft.	13. All pharmacy medicines, all medicinal products on a general sale list and such prescription only medicines which are not for parenteral administration and which have been sold or supplied to the operator or commander of an aircraft in response to an order in writing signed by a doctor.	13. The supply shall be only so far as is necessary for the immediate treatment of sick or injured persons on the aircraft and, in the case of a prescription only medicine, shall be in accordance with the written instructions of a doctor as to the circumstances in which the prescription only medicines of the description in question are to be used on the aircraft.
14. Persons employed as qualified first-aid personnel on offshore installations.	14. All medicinal products.	14. The supply shall be only so far as is necessary for the treatment of persons on the installation.
15. A prison officer.	15. All medicinal products on the general sale list.	15. The supply shall only be so far as is necessary for the treatment of prisoners.
16. Persons who hold a certificate in first aid from the Mountain Rescue Council of England and Wales, or from the Northern Ireland Mountain Rescue Co-ordinating Committee.	16. All pharmacy medicines, all medicinal products on a general sale list and such prescription only medicines which are sold or supplied to a person specified in column 1 of this paragraph in response to an order in writing signed by a doctor.	16. The supply shall be only so far as is necessary for the treatment of sick or injured persons in the course of providing mountain rescue services.
17. Her Majesty's armed forces.	17. All medicinal products.	17. The supply shall be only so far as is necessary for the treatment of a sick or injured person or the prevention of ill-health.
18. A person ("P") carrying on the business of a school who is trained to administer the relevant medicine.	18. A prescription only medicinal product comprising an inhaler containing salbutamol.	18. The supply shall be— (a) in the course of P carrying on the business of a school; (b) where supply is to a pupil at that school who is known to suffer from asthma; and (c) where the pupil requires the medicinal product in an emergency.

(1) 1990 c.16. Section 27 was amended by the Local Government etc (Scotland) Act 1994 section 180(1) and Schedule 18 paragraph 163 (3), the Food Standards Act 1999 section 40(1) and Schedule 5 paragraphs 7 and 8, the Local Government (Wales) Act 1994 section 22(3) and Schedule 9 paragraph 16(2), S.I. 1994/865 regulation 24, and the Local Government and Public Involvement in Health Act 2007 sections 22 and 241, Schedule 1 Part 2 paragraph 17, and Schedule 18 Part 1.

(2) 1991 No. 762 (N.I. 7). There are amendments not relevant to these Regulations.

(3) 1990 c.16.

(4) 1989 No. 846 (N.I. 6).

(5) 2006 c. 41.

(6) 1978 c. 29.

(7) 2006 c. 42.

(8) S.I. 1972/1265 (N.I. 14).

(9) S.I. 2001/3998, to which there are amendments that are not relevant.

(10) S.R. 2002 No. 1, to which there are amendments that are not relevant.

(11) S.I. 2001/3998 as amended by S.I. 2007/2154. There are other amendments that are not relevant.

(12) S.R. 2002 No. 1, as amended by S.R. 2007 No. 348. There are other amendments that are not relevant.

(13) 1970 c.40: subsection (1) was amended by section 272(1) of and Schedule 30 to the Local Government Act 1972; section 16 of and Schedule 8 paragraph 15 to the Local Government Act 1985, and section 66(6) and (8) of, and Schedule 16 paragraph 38(5) and Schedule 18 to the Local Government (Wales) Act 1994. Subsection (1A) was inserted by section 66(6) of and Schedule 16 paragraph 38 (5) to that Act. Subsection 2 was substituted by section 180(1) of and Schedule 13 paragraph 85(2) to the Local Government etc (Scotland) Act 1994, and subsection (7) was repealed by sections 1 (1) and 194 of, and Schedule 1 paragraph 8 and Schedule 34 Part 1 to the Local Government, Planning and Land Act 1980.

Appendix 3

In March 2014 the European Commission published a question and answer document responding to frequently asked questions in relation to the guidelines on Good Distribution Practice of medicinal products for human use. This document sets out frequently asked 'questions and answers' regarding the new guidelines on Good Distribution Practice of medicinal products for human use applicable as of 8 September 2013[1] and their revision of November 2013[2].

It should be noted that the views expressed in this questions and answers document are not legally binding. Ultimately, only the European Court of Justice can give an authoritative interpretation of Union law.

1. QUESTION: IN CHAPTER 2 – PERSONNEL, 2.3.(1), WHAT IS THE DEFINITION OF "COMPETENT"?

Answer: Having the necessary experience and/or training to adequately perform the job.

2. QUESTION: CONCERNING CHAPTER 2 – PERSONNEL, 2.4 (1), IS IT POSSIBLE TO EMPLOY STAFF STARTING THEIR PROFESSIONAL CAREER?

Answer: Yes, if you properly training them before assigning them to their tasks.

3. QUESTION: IN CHAPTER 2 – PERSONNEL, 2.4.(5), WHAT IS MEANT BY "PERIODICALLY ASSESSED"?

Answer: Assessed at regular intervals. The timing of intervals is left flexible, without prejudice to national legislation.

---

[1] Guidelines of 7 March 2013 on Good Distribution Practice of Medicinal Products for Human Use, OJ C 68, 8.3.2013, p. 1.

[2] Guidelines of 5 November 2013 on Good Distribution Practice of Medicinal Products for Human Use, OJ C 343, 23.11.2013, p. 1.

4. QUESTION: IN CHAPTER 2 – PERSONNEL, 2.5, DOES THE STATEMENT "APPROPRIATE PROCEDURES RELATING TO PERSONNEL HYGIENE, RELEVANT TO THE ACTIVITIES BEING CARRIED OUT, SHOULD BE ESTABLISHED AND OBSERVED" REFER TO THE HEALTH AND/OR CLEANLINESS OF THE STAFF?

Answer: It only refers to the cleanliness of the staff, so to avoid any alteration of the product.

5. QUESTION: IN CHAPTER 3 – PREMISES AND EQUIPMENT, 3.2.(3), IS THE INTENT OF SEGREGATION TO AVOID "CROSS-CONTAMINATION" AS MENTIONED IN CHAPTER 5?

Answer: The intent of this provision is to avoid handling errors and accidental swaps of products. This is why electronic segregation is allowed, except for falsified, expired, recalled and rejected products which always have to be segregated physically.

6. QUESTION: CONCERNING CHAPTER 3 – PREMISES AND EQUIPMENT, 3.2.(7), IS THE LID OF A BOX / TOTE AN ADEQUATE PROTECTION AGAINST WEATHER CONDITIONS?

Answer: Any tool protecting products from prevailing weather conditions is acceptable.

7. QUESTION: CONCERNING CHAPTER 3 – PREMISES AND EQUIPMENT, 3.2.1, HOW MANY PROBES ARE NECESSARY TO MONITOR THE TEMPERATURE?

Answer: The number of probes and their placement depend on the risk analysis performed on the site and the placement should be in agreement with the mapping results.

8. QUESTION: CONCERNING CHAPTER 3 – PREMISES AND EQUIPMENT, 3.2.1.(2), WHAT IS MEANT BY INITIAL TEMPERATURE MAPPING?

Answer: An initial temperature mapping is an exercise in which temperature sensors are placed on the points identified as most critical through a risk analysis (e.g. at different heights, near a sunny window, next to the doors, etc.). Once placed, a measurement is taken over a period of time and with the results obtained, the temperature sensors will be places where greater fluctuation occurred. The mapping should be performed in different seasons where highest and lowest temperatures are reached.

EUROPEAN COMMISSION
Q&A ON GDP GUIDELINES

9. QUESTION: CONCERNING CHAPTER 3 – PREMISES AND EQUIPMENT, 3.3.(3), WHAT ARE APPROPRIATE SETTINGS FOR THE ALARM LEVELS?

Answer: Alarm settings should be chosen as to guarantee a timely alert of personnel when there are excursions from predefined storage conditions.

10. QUESTION: CONCERNING CHAPTER 3 – PREMISES AND EQUIPMENT, 3.3.2.(1), IS IT REQUIRED TO HAVE ONLY EQUIPMENT WITH A CE CERTIFICATE OF CONFORMITY?

Answer: No. The CE marking is mandatory only for products dating from 1993 or later. It should be noted that the presence of a CE certificate of Conformity doesn't exempt from equipment validation/qualification.

11. QUESTION: CONCERNING CHAPTER 3 – PREMISES AND EQUIPMENT, 3.3.2.(1), IS IT REQUIRED TO RECORD ALL DEVIATIONS OR CAN THEY BE LIMITED TO SIGNIFICANT DEVIATIONS HAVING AN IMPACT ON PRODUCT SECURITY AND INTEGRITY?

Answer: All deviations from established procedures should be documented.

12. QUESTION: CONCERNING CHAPTER 5 – OPERATIONS, 5.3 (3), ARE THERE ANY BEST PRACTICES FOR THE INVESTIGATION OF "UNUSUAL SALES PATTERNS"?

Answer: It is recommended to check for unusual repetition of orders, sudden increases of orders, and unusually low prices.

13. QUESTION: CONCERNING CHAPTER 5 – OPERATIONS, 5.4 (3), HOW CAN WHOLESALERS PROVE THAT THE MEDICINES THEY RECEIVE ARE RELEASED FOR SALE?

Answer: The batches of medicinal products which have undergone the controls referred to in Art. 51 of Directive 2001/83/EC in a Member State are exempt from the controls if they are marketed in another Member State accompanied by the control reports signed by the qualified person. In other words, the batch arriving from another member state needs to be accompanied by evidence that the manufacturer's qualified person has certified the finished product batch for the target member state. The technical means by which this evidence is provided has been left to the discretion of the companies: a physical control report or an equivalent system of proof of release.

14. QUESTION: CONCERNING CHAPTER 5 – OPERATIONS, 5.4. (3), CAN THE PROVISION REQUIRING WHOLESALERS TO PROVE THAT THE MEDICINES THEY RECEIVE ARE RELEASED FOR SALE BE MADE APPLICABLE AS OF 2017, WHEN MEDICINAL PRODUCTS WILL CARRY SAFETY FEATURES THAT CAN BE CHECKED THROUGH A DATABASE?

Answer: No, these provisions are already into operation as the new GDP guideline simply repeats what mentioned in Directive 2001/83/EC.

15. QUESTION: IN CHAPTER 5 – OPERATIONS, 5.5.(1), WHAT IS THE DEFINITION OF "SEPARATELY"?

Answer: This provision refers to physical separation only in case of presence of other products likely to alter the medicinal product. Segregation is also necessary for falsified, expired, recalled and rejected medicines. In all other cases, electronic segregation is possible.

16. QUESTION: CONCERNING CHAPTER 5 – OPERATIONS, 5.5. (8), IN WHAT WAY SHOULD INVESTIGATION AND DOCUMENTATION BE DONE?

Answer: Reasons for stock irregularities should be investigated and documented.

17. QUESTION: CONCERNING CHAPTER 6 – COMPLAINTS, RETURNS, SUSPECTED FALSIFIED MEDICINAL PRODUCTS AND MEDICINAL PRODUCT RECALLS, 6.3.(2)(I), HOW CAN WHOLESALERS VERIFY THAT A PACK HAS NOT BEEN OPENED IF IT DOES NOT CARRY AN ANTI-TAMPER DEVICE?

Answer: The anti-tampering device will become compulsory in the coming years. Meanwhile, check to the best of your capacities whether the pack has signs of tampering.

18. QUESTION: CONCERNING CHAPTER 6 – COMPLAINTS, RETURNS, SUSPECTED FALSIFIED MEDICINAL PRODUCTS AND MEDICINAL PRODUCT RECALLS, 6.3.(2)(III), HOW SHOULD THE CUSTOMER DEMONSTRATE THAT THE MEDICINAL PRODUCTS HAVE BEEN TRANSPORTED, STORED AND HANDLED IN COMPLIANCE WITH SPECIFIC STORAGE REQUIREMENTS?

Answer: The customer needs to provide papers showing that the medicinal products have been transported, stored and handled in compliance with their specific storage requirements.

19. QUESTION: CONCERNING CHAPTER 6 – COMPLAINTS RETURNS, SUSPECTED FALSIFIED MEDICINAL PRODUCTS AND MEDICINAL PRODUCT RECALLS, 6.3.(3), WHAT SHOULD THE DOCUMENTED EVIDENCE CONTAIN TO BE REGARDED AS SUFFICIENT?

Answer: The evidence should cover:
(i)   delivery to customer;
(ii)   examination of the product;
(iii)   opening of the transport packaging;
(iv)   return of the product to the packaging;
(v)   collection and return to the distributor;
(vi)   return to the distribution site refrigerator.

20. QUESTION: IN CHAPTER 6 – COMPLAINTS, RETURNS SUSPECTED FALSIFIED MEDICINAL PRODUCTS AND MEDICINAL PRODUCT RECALLS, 6.3.(3)(IV), DOES THE TERM "PACKAGING" REFER TO THE TRANSPORT BOX?

Answer: Yes

21. QUESTION: IN CHAPTER 6 – COMPLAINTS, RETURNS SUSPECTED FALSIFIED MEDICINAL PRODUCTS AND MEDICINAL PRODUCT RECALLS, 6.5.(6), WHAT DOES IT MEAN TO RECORD THE PROGRESS OF THE RECALL?

Answer: You need to record the status of the recall and whether it was successful or not.

22. QUESTION: CONCERNING CHAPTER 9 – TRANSPORTATION 9.2.(1), CAN WE DEVIATE FROM STORAGE CONDITIONS IF THE MANUFACTURER AGREES TO THE TRANSPORTATION OF THE PRODUCT WITHIN A CERTAIN TEMPERATURE RANGE (2°-25°C FOR A LIMITED TIME FRAME OF 6 HOURS?

Answer: No. Storage temperature limits as described by the manufacturer or on the outer packaging need to be respected for each stage of transport during the whole transport chain.

23. QUESTION: CONCERNING CHAPTER 9 – TRANSPORTATION, 9.2.(9), ARE TRANSPORTATION COMPANIES REQUIRED TO HOLD A WHOLESALE DISTRIBUTION AUTHORISATION AND COMPLY WITH GDP?

Answer: Transport companies do not need to hold a wholesale distribution authorisation to transport medicinal products. However they should follow the parts of the GDP guideline relevant to their activities, amongst others Chapter 9.

24. QUESTION: IN CHAPTER 9 – TRANSPORTATION, 9.4.(2), DOES THE DEFINITION OF HIGHLY ACTIVE MATERIAL COMPRISE CYTOSTATICS?

Answer: The guidelines do not include a list of highly active materials, or a definition of highly active material. Without prejudice to specific provisions included in national legislation, the wording leaves a margin of manoeuvre to the manufacturer/distributor.

25. QUESTION: IN CHAPTER 9 – TRANSPORTATION 9.4.(7), WHAT IS THE DEFINITION OF "CHILLED"?

Answer: "Chilled" refers to refrigerated storage conditions.

Index